Wanted—Le:
A study of Negro deve

Theodore DeBose Bratton

Alpha Editions

This edition published in 2024

ISBN 9789362998439

Design and Setting By
Alpha Editions
www.alphaedis.com
Email - info@alphaedis.com

As per information held with us this book is in Public Domain.
This book is a reproduction of an important historical work.
Alpha Editions uses the best technology to reproduce historical work
in the same manner it was first published to preserve its original nature.
Any marks or number seen are left intentionally to preserve.

Contents

CHAPTER I THE NEGRO IN AFRICA	- 1 -
CHAPTER II THE NEGRO IN LIBERIA	- 16 -
CHAPTER III THE NEGRO IN HAITI	- 34 -
CHAPTER IV THE SLAVE AND THE FREEDMAN IN AMERICA	- 52 -
CHAPTER V THE PERIOD OF WAR AND RECONSTRUCTION	- 73 -
CHAPTER VI THE EDUCATION OF THE NEGRO	- 85 -
FOOTNOTES:	- 104 -
CHAPTER VII THE CHRISTIAN DEVELOPMENT OF THE NEGRO IN AMERICA	- 105 -
FOOTNOTES:	- 129 -
CHAPTER VIII WHAT OF THE FUTURE?	- 131 -
APPENDIX	- 144 -
NOTE 1	- 144 -
NOTE 2	- 145 -
NOTE 4	- 146 -
NOTE 5	- 148 -
NOTE 6	- 150 -
NOTE 7	- 155 -
NOTE 8	- 156 -
NOTE 9	- 157 -
NOTE 10	- 157 -
NOTE 11	- 158 -
NOTE 12	- 159 -

NOTE 13 - 160 -

NOTE 14 - 161 -

Chapter I
THE NEGRO IN AFRICA

The Africa of five hundred years ago, when the modern nations first dipped into its wild and troubled life, presented at least as great a variety of racial characteristics as any other continent. Natural barriers; climatic influences; the recurring desert, swamp, and prairie areas;—all tended to segregate the tribes, and to fix widely different physical characteristics. The ancient Empires of the Mediterranean had left the posterity of their mixed families, and the tradition of their mingled religions, on the borders of that great sea. Inevitably these exercised more or less of influence on the backward people to the South of them, tingeing their blood, their characteristics, and their religion, though in a way difficult to define and to a degree which baffles measurement. Where effects have been in the making for many centuries and are remote from the causes, the links between them are not easily traceable. It is only in modern times that Mohammedanism, for example, has pushed its conquests much below the great desert region. In the time of the slave traffic, the Mediterranean influence must have penetrated to only a comparatively short distance up the Nile and down the western coast, while very gradually diffusing itself through the north Sudan area. In general, we may approach the study of the Negro in Africa with little thought of this outside influence, noting it only where marked traces are discovered either from ancient or modern sources.

Various students of the negro peoples have divided them into families; but the divisions vary, and no fixed terminology has become so dominant as to command common consent. For our purpose, the four Families hereafter described comprise the African Negroes. A minute study of these families will reveal many tribal subdivisions, each with distinguishing traits—physical, mental and moral—developed by environment, and yet plainly traceable to common family origins. Such a minute study is not our purpose, and we shall limit our view to the four Families in whose development we are especially interested.

I. The Negrito Family. In this Family are three distinct though kindred tribes—the Pygmies, the Bushmen, and the Hottentots—supposed to be the original inhabitants of Africa. As these tribes are only remotely represented in America, they may be dismissed with short notice.

They are all of small stature, ranging in height from four to five feet, and are early mentioned by the Greek and Roman historians, whose stories of the dwarf Pygmies were treated as traveller's tales until the discoveries of the eighteenth and nineteenth centuries proved the so-called fables of Homer, Aristotle, and Pliny to be true. From the nomadic, forest-dwelling Pygmies of central Africa, with their low mental and social development, there is a distinct advance in their nearest kinsmen, the Bushmen of the desert regions scattered throughout this same area. Among them, music is a distinct form of expression, and they exhibit a degree of artistic ability in the depicting of animal figures and even of scenes from their marauding life. More developed still, are the Hottentots of the South. In mental and moral character, as well as in mechanical ingenuity, they surpass their kinsmen. Language is still meager in power of expression, but the Hottentot *kraal* or village community represents a much higher stage of social life than is found among the Pygmies or the Bushmen. Religiously, too, the Hottentot is on a higher plane than the related tribes.

The effect of European settlement in the land of the Bushmen and Hottentots has been disastrous to these wild people. Dr. Bryce says, "Along the south bank of the Orange River and to the north of it, small tribes, substantially identical with the Hottentots, still wander over the arid wilderness. But in the settled parts of the colony, the Hottentot, of whom we used to hear so much, and, at one time, feared so much, has vanished more completely than has the Red Indian from the Atlantic States of America." The Pygmies are still remote from the white man's influence. Is it this alone that saves them from a like fate?

II. The Sudan Family. These occupy almost the entire Sudan country, which is the widest part of Africa, south of the Sahara Desert, and extends from the Atlantic Ocean to the Abyssinian highlands on the east. "The whole Sudan is full of animal excitement. There is never a dull hour for man or beast. All is conflict, noise and motion. Even at night there is no repose or solitude." Most of the great rivers have their source in this region, in which also are found many lakes teeming with life. Over much of this area, nature provides all the necessities of life; literally so, since clothing is not so classed, the climate favoring the unchanging garb of nature.

The Sudan country is divided into geographical zones named after the chief product of each. The equatorial and torrid belt—the so-called Banana Zone—abounds in fruits as well as game; next above is the Millet Zone, with its combined trees and grain-fields, millet, sorghum, etc., providing edible vegetation corresponding to our wheat, corn, and rice; next above is the Cattle Zone, a prairie-country, rich in grasses, its fertile lands inviting agricultural pursuits; above this, and blending into the Sahara Desert, is the Camel Zone of which no further mention need be made.

The estimated 80,000,000 people of the Sudan Family are divided into three fairly distinct types: (1) The Negritians, a primitive and numerous negro race which claims our chief interest because it provided most of our American Negroes. (2) The Fellatahs, a mixture of Negritian and Berber, the latter a branch of the Hamitic family. This mingling has produced a fairly distinct ruling class. (3) The Arab toward the eastern section of the Sudan, who also intermingled with the Negritians, and became the ruling class of the region to the eastward.

Each of these types, with its many tribes, inhabits sections of the three climatic or geographical zones of the Sudan—the so-called Banana, Millet, and Cattle Zones—and, since the climate and products of the zones determine the main characteristics of the people, we follow the zones in studying the people.

The characteristics of life, as well as the industries, everywhere vary with the changing physical geography of a people's habitat; it is natural, therefore, to find a general and decided ascent in industrial life from the tropical Banana Zone up to the more temperate Millet, and again up to the Cattle Zone.

(1) The hot, humid atmosphere of the Banana Zone, and the abundant, never-failing fruits of nature supplied without the necessity of human culture, have developed a thriftless people, in whom the absence of food-problems has bred an hereditary distaste for exertion of any kind. Here and there may be found patches of corn, yams, and ground nuts, planted by the women and slaves, and requiring little culture. Fishing, perhaps the most leisurely of all sports, is indulged in; but hunting is little followed, human flesh being preferred; for the people of this zone are cannibals. The making of implements of warfare is probably done by the men; but, where slavery is the habit, no doubt most manual labor is the task of the slaves—the booty of war which seems to be the chief pastime.

Polygamy is universal, family life is loose, and the standards of chastity are correspondingly low. Wives are bought or captured; and, since frequent wars lessen the male population, women are numerous and cheap. The prevailing standard is unmoral rather than immoral. Chastity is a matter of respecting the property of others, and unchastity is punished because it is a violation of this respect for private property. Women are always property, first of their parents, and then of their husbands or owners.

(2) Passing northward into the Millet Zone, the tropical forests give place to alternate woods and prairies which commence at about the 11th parallel of north latitude. Here is the great agricultural region, grains and nut trees taking the place of the fruits and shrubs. In addition, cotton for clothing and other uses has been grown for many centuries, though, until recent years, for domestic consumption only. Domestic animals—cattle, sheep, asses, pigs, etc.—are in use, and wild animals and birds abound. The

latter are both a source of food and also of peril; and, in the crop-season, slaves are employed to save the produce from enemies on land and in air. The problem of life in the Millet Zone is far more difficult than in the Banana, for man must labor for his food, till the soil, and store up the crops. In many places wells must be dug through solid rock to supply water for men, domestic animals, and fowls. In still others, wood must be hauled over long distances.

Necessity has stimulated quite a remarkable development of the industrial arts. Potters and carpenters fashion urns and bins for storing and protecting grain and other produce. Smiths smelt iron, with charcoal as the fuel; make hoes, axes, knives, and other utensils. Leather workers dress and dye hides, fashioning them into shoes, cloaks, shields, water-vessels, etc. In one district, the people have learned to make and to color glass; in another, to manufacture soap. The weaving of cotton cloth and dyeing have been practiced for many centuries.

All the arts, agricultural and industrial, declined during the flourishing days of the slave-trade, when the selling of captive slaves furnished the conquerors an easy road to wealth and to the possession of much that their own labor alone had formerly provided. Gold is an important commodity and, stored in quills, is used as a medium of exchange; but, strangely enough, it seems only in more modern times to have been fashioned into coins.

The labor is divided into well-defined crafts. Besides those already mentioned, there are tailors, musicians, architects who are also builders, barbers who also extract teeth, and even manicurists. Slave-labor is much in demand; for here, as throughout the world, until modern times, wherever agricultural and mechanical industries flourished, slavery has prevailed. And just as the ancient and modern monarchies have depended upon force of arms to supply the slaves needed, so has it been with the negro monarchies.

Professor Ely, in his *Political Economy*, argues, from this universal practice doubtless, that slavery is both right and wrong. "There is a time in human development when slavery represents a step in human progress, the best and longest that men were able to take. Such a step is always right. It is wrong, when men have learned how to do better." Upon this view of the case, a host of African explorers and observers have testified to what they regard as the obvious advantages of the well-nigh universal slave-system of the more progressive tribes. They testify, too, to its partially patriarchal character in the agricultural regions, where the use of slaves, as sacrifices to the gods or offerings upon the death of a king, is practically never found. As an offset, however, to this rather roseate picture, is the even more general witness to the fact that slaves in this zone run away whenever opportunity offers, and, if chance favors them, well supplied with the goods and cattle of their masters to comfort them along the way.

The family life of the Millet Zone is decidedly above the standard of the more tropical tribes. Doubtless the possession of property for which much labor has been expended, and the necessity to preserve and to protect it, make for a higher sense of the duties which the relations of life bring. The women are more nearly equal in number with the men, and are relatively more valuable, so that a substantial price must be paid for a wife. The more complicated life, involving barns, storehouses, etc., enlarges the idea of a home and family. The care of the domestic animals leads up to the care of the home inmates, and furniture is more plentiful and comfortable. The settled life is far more favorable than the nomadic to the accumulation of household needs and comforts. Life is both more complex and more expensive. So, in this zone, polygamy gives place to monogamy save in the case of the kings and the rich, who seem to accumulate wives with wealth. The stable life tends to strengthen the ties between parents and children.

(3) The Cattle Zone, north of the Millet, is generally an open prairie, in which trees are scarce and grass abundant. Here, cattle and horses abound, many of the former in a wild state, and sheep and goats thrive. The industries of the Zone also include, to a limited extent, agriculture and manufacturing. Cattle constitute the wealth of the country; goats furnish the milk; rice, sweet potatoes, and a variety of vegetables are the staple foods; cotton and indigo are raised both for home consumption and for trading.

The city of Timbuctoo is one of the commercial centers of this Zone. Here quantities of products are exchanged—linen and cotton cloth, shoes of an ancient pattern, and saddles; iron and copper implements, woodenware, pottery, etc., and great numbers of cattle.

Slavery furnishes the greater part of the labor in the Cattle Zone; and here as in the Millet Zone, the slaves generally occupy the position of serfs to a chief.

Family life is at a decidedly higher stage of development. While wives are bought, and at a high price, there is a notable exception in the case of one tribe, according to whose customs daughters are allowed the right to be wooed, and the privilege of accepting or rejecting the suitor. Here only, among the many tribes of Negritians, there is evidence of romantic love so inseparable from marriage in our own land. In this Zone not a few of the tribes are Mohammedans, and in these the customs of sex relations and family life are largely dominated by that religion.

Where the Fellatahs dominate, the cleavage between rich and poor is very marked, the homes of the former being sometimes almost palatial, while those of the poor are miserable hovels made of poles, often with sorghum stalks for rafters, and straw mats for covering, and side-walls. A variety of architecture and material, however, appears in the many villages and cities of the Zone, and the daily sweeping of floors shows a desire for cleanliness unknown to other zones. The men are the chief supporters of their families, and woman enjoys a liberty elsewhere universally denied her. She owns her own property ofttimes; and her own slaves, if the family be rich, to cultivate and garner her crops. The wife is treated with respect, yet is humble and submissive, kneeling in obeisance to her husband.

Politically, the governments of the Sudan present much the picture of the old feudal days of our own ancestors. The king is supreme, and in him all legislative power is vested, influenced by the local chiefs of the towns into which the inhabitants are gathered for purposes of protection. Under the king, a council and chief officers execute his commands. Each town is administered by its local chief, who is supreme in his district. All alike furnish soldiers for the king's army, and pay tribute to the royal treasury. Below the aristocratic class are the freemen; and below them the slaves, in castes which inhibit all incentive to rise in the social scale. However crude, a system of laws is administered, and trials are conducted by the local chief or by one of the king's officers. Appeal can be made to the king in case decisions are felt to be unjust. Penalties are irregular, but generally extreme, including beheading or burning or dismemberment in the case of murder, while severe whipping with rawhide suffices for lesser offenses.

The remaining two great Families—the Gallas and the Bantus—inhabit eastern and southeastern Africa. They are not so largely represented in America as their kinsmen already mentioned, and regretfully we must pass them by with short notice of each.

III. The Gallas inhabit the region known as Nubia, lying to the south and west of Abyssinia, and the region on the two sides of the White Nile and thence southward almost to Lake Victoria. But it must be borne in mind that these divisional names are arbitrarily bestowed upon large groups, comprising millions of people, divided into scores of tribes, each more or less distinct in size, color, and social customs. The northern group of tribes have sometimes been called Nubians. Some of these, in time, became mixed with the Hamites, and, in ancient times, were dangerous enemies of the Roman Province of Africanus, and even compelled Diocletian to withdraw his garrisons from above the cataracts of the Nile.

About 550 A. D. they were converted to Christianity and welded into a great people under the leadership of Silko. With the coming of the Arabs, they were gradually subdued, partly by force, still more by amalgamation; and, by the fourteenth century, they became largely Mohammedan in religion, while remaining essentially Negro in spite of Arab and Bosnian infusions. They have oval faces, large black eyes, and prominent narrow noses; in color, they are dark mahogany or bronze. Their kinsmen to the East and South are very similar in color and feature; and both are fine, sturdy types, the women often exceedingly graceful. Their social and economic life is not unlike that of the pastoral and agricultural tribes of the Sudan.

The tribes farther south are of a still lighter color, some being an earthy red, while others, the Mangbattu for example, are of a lighter tint than perhaps any other tribe of Africa.

IV. The Bantus inhabit the vast area from about Lake Victoria, comprising Eastern Equatorial and South Central Africa. Of the Equatorial tribes, the Ugandas are generally the finest types and the most progressive. Stanley tells us that he found them to be fine craftsmen. Even more than elsewhere, Uganda is a land of musicians, who have developed a great variety of native musical instruments. The Congo region also produces a fine race, physically superior to any of their kinsmen. In the mountains of the region "one sees magnificent specimens of human beings, both male and female. They are a tall, powerful people of dark brown color, often with regular features."

The tribes to the south of the Equator are among the very finest in general physical and mental development; among them are the Zulus, the Kaffirs, and others nearly as well known to the general reader. The Zulus, e. g., are tall, shapely and muscular, and often with Grecian features, the skin varying from a light clear brown to blue black. Some of these tribes are highly developed in foresight, self-control, rational interpretation, and general intelligence. Many are fearless and brave to the point of foolhardiness, and the stories of the achievements of some of their warriors read like the tales of the Scottish chiefs so fascinating to our boyhood.

But we must content ourselves now with these brief comments, adding a quotation from *The Mind of Primitive Man*, by Boas. "To those unfamiliar with the products of native African art and industry, a walk through one of the large museums of Europe would be a revelation. None of our American museums has made collections that exhibit this subject in any way worth while. The blacksmith, the wood carver, the weaver, the potter—these all produce ware original in form, executed with care, and exhibiting that love of labor and interest in the results of work, which are apparently so often lacking among the Negroes in our American surroundings."

Our studies have revealed, in the negro race, a great variety of intelligence, often of a very high order; powers of organization of no slight degree of development; and thrift that has supplied large cities as trade centers, of which Timbuctoo is, perhaps, chief. "Neither is the wisdom of the philosopher absent," says Professor Boas. "A perusal of any of the collections of African proverbs that have been published, will demonstrate the homely, practical philosophy of the Negro, which is often proof of sound feeling and judgment."

The religions of the more advanced tribes, though differing in many of their practical details of application to life, may fairly be treated as one. It should not surprise us to find that there is no known tribe in Africa, or elsewhere in the world, which has not a religion; for God "hath not left Himself without witness" among any people.

Religion does not begin with the Incarnate Christ. He is not the first revelation of God, but His last and complete revelation. Through the personal message of the Incarnate One correcting errors, interpreting and confirming mysteries, and thus revealing the rational in what is inexplicable and indefinable otherwise, comes the interpretation of man's natural religion. The fulfilment of all religion is Jesus Christ; without Whom, religion has ever degenerated into superstition. In its primary meaning, Religion is the law of relation—personal relation to all that is outside of self—to God, to one's own complex nature, to man, and to the world. And since the law of relation is personal, it is susceptible of an infinite variety of interpretations and applications as personality grows and expands. Upon the growth of the religious sense, therefore, depends the progress of moral and spiritual character. The source of enlightenment for the savage is the great Book of Nature, God's first volume of His Self-revelation. In the interpretation of this book, manifold elements enter, combining to yield many lessons from its living chapters. The initial question of all peoples as they looked out upon the world has been: Whence came it? And upon the forces of nature: What are they? In a land filled with wild beasts and reptiles, visited by storms and floods, subject to earthquakes and volcanoes, its people a prey to disease and death, what is the explanation that the African has given? What has he thought of sun, moon and stars, and of earth itself? It is safe to say that his answers to these questions have been pretty much what other primitive peoples have given. If the wind blows, it is a spirit grown restless; if the lightning flashes, it is the angry hiss of a malignant spirit; if sun and moon travel through the air, they are powerful gods, far removed, but remotely affecting the earth; if an eclipse comes, the gods in anger hide their faces; if wild beasts roar and serpents hiss, these are the emissaries of evil spirits. Thus everything that moves is endowed with life and intelligence. The Eskimo, for instance, is persuaded that a watch is a living thing because its parts move.

Naturally, the African first feared the mysterious living spirits; then sought to pacify and bribe by the only offerings valuable in his own eyes— the food and drink which satisfied and made content. His idea of spirits was the reflection of his scant knowledge of himself—a half-true, half-false, canon of interpretation which becomes wholly false when the other half is unknown or forgotten; for the idea of self must also be the reflection of God's knowledge of us and of His purpose for us and our knowledge of Him.

In many tribes, a belief in a double personality prevails, and this the African proves by the wandering of oneself when, in the dream of sleep, he goes upon journeys, meets friends or enemies, engages in sports, or conflict, and returns, filled with experiences, to the other self which has been quietly asleep all the while. And because this dream-self meets, sometimes, the spirits of the dead, therefore one of these selves must live after death. This gives rise, too, to the belief that one of these personal spirits is not inseparable from the body, but may go out at pleasure at any time, and inhabit other men, or even beasts. This spirit, or *Kra*, makes its exit through the mouth always, and since these Kras are moving about at large, a strange Kra may slip into the unoccupied place of another, and cause no end of mischief; it is important, therefore, not to sleep with the mouth open.

When a man loses his Kra, illness results, and the witch doctor must be called in, who brings a good Kra, or dream-soul, in a basket. If successful in getting this new Kra into the sick man's mouth, recovery results. So, too, when the Kra of the dead lingers about the home, sickness is caused, and only the doctor, by inducing the Kra to move on to the land of the dead, can thus restore the living to health. In time, however, among many tribes, the Kra returns to make his abode in a newborn infant, whose features and actions disclose the identity of the Kra. Miss Kingsley notes the incident of an identification. When a baby has grasped a pipe shown him, the mother is sure that "he is Uncle John. See, he knows his pipe!" The reader may find some correspondence between this notion of the double personality and those entertained by the scholarly psychologists of the Caucasian race in their dissertation upon the supra-normal self, and like manifestations.

This feature has been dwelt upon because it serves to convey the point of view of the Negro, surrounded by the spirits of gods and devils and dead men, and living too; and the spirits of every life and force of Nature,—a perfect swarm of spirits, nearly all of whom are busy meddling with the affairs of men, and who must be outwitted or bribed or won over if disaster is to be avoided. Life is thus a tragic drama unending, whose comedy, however, is constantly realized in the outwitting of the cunning spirits, and the overcoming of the powerful by ingenious strategy.

Every tribe has a secret society, through which every freeman must pass. In the course of this education, should a boy be found who can see spirits, he is assigned to the medical profession, and is apprenticed to a witch-doctor to whom a good fee must be paid, and who instructs him in the mysteries of the spirit-world. He accompanies his teacher, picks up his bedside manner, learns to howl in a professional way, and, if possible, how to simulate epilepsy. A knowledge, also of the dispositions of the prospective patients, their financial standing, the scandals of the people, is of great value to the budding doctor. Perhaps this method of practice may seem absurd; but, in spite of this, many of the doctors possess a fund of wisdom in dealing with human nature, and also a store of knowledge of medical herbs, which has been of great value in later times to the white explorers and missionaries, as well as to the Negroes. According to the lights which they possess, they are guided often by the same motives which sway the civilized physician, and apply the same method of investigation employed by the enlightened scientist. The most that should be said is that the African doctor is behind the times. Yet, even here, it is interesting to know, and simple justice to Africa to repeat the record, that for many centuries men of the Yoruba tribe have known that smallpox is produced by the evil god *Shank-panna* whose agents are *mosquitoes and flies*; and there are not a few examples of doctors who examine their patients, locate the disease by scientific diagnosis, and prescribe both diet and medicine. In general terms, "religion and medicine" are one and the same in the mind of the African, since all medical practice is contact with the spirits.

A priestly caste, consisting of three orders, prevails in some of these tribes. Each order represents a class of gods. Their office is hereditary, but is replenished through the secret society of the tribe which forms a school of training for the priest, as for the doctor. Idols are much used, to whom sacrifices are offered in worship of the god represented.

The very high development in aesthetics is so conspicuous a characteristic of the Negro as to make a racial differentiation. No other race is so musical, no other more given to dancing, no other so profuse in personal decorations.

The boatman sings all day long, keeping time with his paddle; the woman pounds grain in time with her chants; the farmer, with his hoe. Joy, grief, love, pain, are all expressed in spontaneous song. In some regions, professional musicians chant the chronicles of their tribes. Sometimes the strolling minstrel sings the folklore, reciting the experiences of men with animals, of animals with animals, acting the parts as he sings the story. In writing of these, Miss Kingsley thus closes her vivid description: "O! that was something like a song! It would have roused a rock to enthusiasm; a civilized audience would have smothered its singer with bouquets!"

Dancing, too, is a mode of expressing feeling, almost universal. Scarcely a night but somewhere in a village the dance is in progress. Among all people, indeed, the bodily expression of inward emotion is the natural ritual of communication. The savage does not find vent for his emotions in the numberless ways acquired by civilized people—through writing, painting, the drama, discoursive language and the like; but he combines them all in the dance, just as at other times they are all expressed in music. It is a mistake to suppose that his dancing is always sensuous and frivolous. There is enough of this, it is true; but at times his deepest emotions are also thus expressed. There is the dance of religious fervor, of preparation for war, of celebration of victory, of lament for loss, in the planting time, and in the harvest. Such dances inspire devotion, courage, industry, patriotism, and tribal unity in a common cause.

But the aesthetics of the Negro are still more vividly and luridly illustrated in his personal decorations, at all times from a sense of beauty, sometimes as tribal insignia. Tattooing, in some tribes; painting, in most of them; the wearing of ornaments on foreheads, in cheeks or lips or ears or nose; the filing of teeth, or even the extraction of one or more, are usual forms of decorations. Body-painting is the practice of the Nile tribes; and, in the west, the dyeing of hands, feet, eyebrows, and lips. Artistic head-dresses and the dyeing of hair seem popular among many tribes. In the cotton area, the use of fancy dyed cloth prevails. The styles are graceful and picturesque. Where straw goods are made, the head-dress is both useful and ornamental a high degree.

A natural question is, to what is the backwardness of the Negro in Africa due? This is not a merely forensic question. To prejudiced people, it is dismissed as a waste of time, since to such people the Negro is incapable of anything better. But prejudice is, of all mental conditions, the least favorable to the satisfactory solution of any question. Our question has had varying answers from many students, among which the following, given in Dowd's *Negro Races*, seems a conservative mean.

"The backwardness of the Negro in Africa is not due directly to lack of mental capacity, but to unfavorable environment. If any other race had peopled Africa in early neolithic times, and remained there until now, it would have advanced no higher than the present culture-level of the Negro."

Africa lies almost wholly in the hot, humid zone of the Tropics, save for the vast Desert of Sahara to the north. There is, indeed, another vast area on the temperate side of the Tropic of Capricorn which, at sight, inspires hope for the development of a rich, virile civilization; but an examination of the isotherms reveals conditions uncongenial to the spontaneous development of a high type of civilization. Even as low as Natal and Cape Colony, the coastal belt produces tropical fruits like all the rest of Africa. In such environs the negro tribes lived in isolation from other races; cut off from the Mediterranean Empire by the Sahara Desert, and from Europe and Asia by the Atlantic and Indian Oceans. Whatever stimulus to development may come from contact with other peoples—and there is much—was denied to the Negro, save that which arose from inter-racial conflict among themselves, an unceasing bar to higher development for any race, and seemingly inseparable from racial isolation.

And yet a distinct progress is clearly manifested through facts which stand out in eloquent boldness. On the one hand, we see the Pygmies, without organization or law or even language save the most meager, with scarce enough even of settled custom to fix any habits of moral life. On the other hand, the most advanced tribes of north and east Africa, like the Yorubas, the Zulus, and the Kaffirs, exhibit a marked degree of progress. Here are well-defined organizations; codes of laws which, however they fall short of ours, are actual codes sufficing for them; moral codes which, however far from the Christian standard, yet form codes to be obeyed and enforced; a language (in the case of the Kaffirs) "adequate for the expression of any ideas whatever"; industries sufficiently developed to meet backward needs; a highly developed aesthetic sense; enough of self-control to conserve courage; and a fair degree of steadfastness of purpose. Among the very highest type, is found the practice of the virtues of affection, kindness, and mutual helpfulness; of honesty in their own group, even to punishing the liar—and much more. Who can gainsay the fact of progress far too great to be overlooked? Who can say what might have been attained under more favorable conditions? Who can say what further progress— slow, very slow, and deliberate—awaits achievements, in view of that which, in the past, has been distinctly and, in many cases, wholly their very own? It is beside our purpose to make a comparison of races. Our study is of the Negro himself; and our findings prove, what naturally would have been expected of God's creation, a people *worth while in themselves.*

What has been the effect of the coming of civilized people to these backward races? The well-nigh universal testimony is proclaimed as a tragic wail, that contact with the white man has, upon the whole, been degrading, not elevating to the Negro. And this is consistently true, though with bright and hopeful exceptions here and there.

From the demoralizing era of the slave-traffic, involving robbing, cheating, the violation of the most solemn treaties, and the bad example of private life, up to the settling of the Congo, the one aim of the white man has been his own profit at whatever cost to the natives. Certain, and often great, advantages to the Negro have been sought and gained by the Christian Church and by scientific efforts; but these are small beside the hurt inflicted by the horde of profit-seeking, selfish fortune-hunters, to whom the Negro is a savage of the lower order, to be tramped upon.

To quote Miss Kingsley again: "It is an unfortunate concomitant of European civilization that its first impress has, almost without exception, been disastrous to the people of lower degree of culture than the European standards. For every sincere bearer of the banner of the Prince of Peace there were a hundred reckless buccaneers, without one thought of the spiritual or physical welfare of the 'savage heathen' whom they met. It is so in the case of Africa. Down both coasts, the European civilization marched, one missionary disposed to recognize the brotherhood of man, and a hundred freebooters insistent that to the victor belong the spoils." Miss Kingsley's language is mild, and is quoted because of its tone.

But happily there is another side here, too, to relieve the tragic gloom of the picture. Concerning the comparatively large endeavors of the Christian missionaries of Uganda in East Africa, and of those on the West Coast, it is most encouraging to be able to quote from Dowd:

"Contact with the Europeans has done much to lift the Waganda (Uganda) from their savagery. It has diminished wars, human sacrifices, trial by ordeal; and has reformed the administration of justice. Many Mission-schools have Christianized and enlightened the masses. It is claimed that 200,000 (this is eight years ago) of the natives can read and write. In religious, as in other innovations, however, the transformation has been too sudden, and not always adapted to native psychology."

This is a mere word about a truly great mission, on a nation-wide scale, whose success constitutes one of the really great romances of modern times. Unhappily, it does not fall to our lot to relate its history, but the reader will miss much if he fails to learn the story as told by the English Church missionaries.

Special attention is called to the closing sentence of the quotation above; for, in it, the finger is put upon the crux of the problem of Christian evangelization, whether in Africa or in America, among the Negroes or the Indians, or wherever one race evangelizes another. When Bishop Tucker of Uganda writes, one feels himself to be at the feet of an expert. "Were I asked," he writes, "to give my opinion as to what, in my estimation, has most hindered the development and independence of the native Churches,

I should unhesitatingly answer, that deep-rooted tendency which there is in the Anglo-Saxon character to Anglicize everything with which it comes in contact." And recently, upon his visit to America, Dr. King, President of the Society for the Propagation of the Gospel, and formerly Bishop of Zanzibar, expressed substantially the same judgment.

The reluctance of the white race, whether in England or America, to permit the negro race to develop his own Christian civilization with all of racial coloring and aesthetic characteristics, has long been restively regarded by many of us. Christianity is not a racial, but a catholic, religion; not obliterating racial characteristics, but regenerating them. A superficial expression of this is the assertion so often made, "religion must adapt itself to peoples." Christianity is a life, and life is not adaptable, it is adoptable. Once adopted, it grows and, therefore, takes form. It is the form that is adaptable; and when the life is permitted to grow normally, it appropriates and consecrates the form that is adaptable to the personality that it inhabits.

Christianity is nowhere and at no time to be *adapted* to anybody; but anybody may be adapted to Christianity, as the power (not the form) of its life transforms and transfuses man. Racial traits and tendencies are so slow to change, that it is a very real question whether they really do change, or whether they are only modified or quickened or redirected with the change of environment which new climes or training, or education produce.

If this be true, the sum total of the process of civilization would be a Caucasian civilization, and a Negro, and an Indian, no matter how much each contributed to the other in the fashioning of his own. Would it not be a great loss to the culture of the human family, if all the races were to lose their predominant characteristics, and were to be reduced to a dead medium level? But, thank God, this is impossible, in spite of the seeming ambition of the Anglo-Saxon to Anglo-Saxonize all peoples, and of the Teuton to Teutonize the world. Statesmen may have been sometimes unfortunate in applying the canon of "self-determination"; but it has its place, in creation, a place which the God of infinite variety has sanctioned.

A glance now, momentary but very earnestly thoughtful, toward the concrete fruits of the Christian Mission to Africa, will throw another ray of light upon our own Mission at home. The picture drawn by close and sympathetic observers is something like the moving picture of a continuous drama. In the beginning, the converted, tutored Negroes were much like children with a new toy among playmates with none. Artificially trained and educated, moulded in a strange pattern, they stood aloof from, and above, their less fortunate old-time fellows, or else reverted to the old type. Vain and prideful in their new attainments, they looked down with contempt upon the uninitiated. This, of course, was not always so; but it was, perhaps, the natural first consequence of a rapid change and too quickly acquired distinction among their own people.

Exceptions there were among the Europeanized Africans, enough to encourage hope of the better day. Some there were who would "no more have dropped their store clothes and gone cannibalizing than we would." And the new day slowly came through the gamut of recurring improvements and relapses which characterizes human progress in every race. There were the isolated leaders, the greater in their day because fashioned without a racial mould, to become by God's grace the ensigns for the gradual gathering of their several peoples.

"Men of large mould, like the Rev. Thomas J. Marshall, of Porto Novo, who was born in one of the blackest spots in darkest Africa, and who has been instrumental in leading a whole people into the knowledge and practice of Christianity; the Rev. Jacob Anaman, a native minister of the Gold Coast, who has been made a fellow of the Royal Geographical Society; Sir Samuel Lewis, Mayor of Freetown, a native of Sierra Leone, who, in 1893, was appointed a companion of the Order of St. Michael and St. George, and was recently distinguished by the Order of Knighthood— the first pure Negro on whom such honor has been conferred. He is an exemplary follower of the Christ. And Bishop Crowther, the first of his race to be called to that sacred office, whose story is known to all the world. Following in his footsteps we have, at the present time, Bishop Phillips and Oluwole, two excellent and worthy natives connected with the Church Missionary Society of the Church of England." And last, there is to be added to this list, Bishop Theophilus Momolu Gardiner, of Liberia, a native Bushman, recently consecrated and charged with the sacred mission of leading his heathen tribe to the foot of the Cross.

These isolated leaders have been and are becoming the forerunners of the many lesser who must be born out of the uplifted population of their tribes. For until the whole population is so far elevated that the few exceptional real leaders are the spontaneous fruit of the tribal tree, real and permanent progress has not yet been made. But then there will be leadership indeed, because it will be recognized as the result of the native Christian life. Such leadership, in fullest sympathy with the life from which it sprang, will arouse enthusiasm, and, in the Master's name and power, draw all men to Him.

Chapter II
THE NEGRO IN LIBERIA

In the previous chapter, attention was called briefly to the effect, upon the Negro races in Africa, of contact with the whites. It was seen that, while the efforts of Christian explorers and missionaries have resulted locally in good to these backward races in their own land, the benefits have been vastly more than offset by the widespread horrors of the white slave-trader and exploiter, and by the harm resulting from the introduction of the liquor and the vices of the white man. But how does it fare with the Negro when his contact with the white race is elsewhere than in Africa? Or what is the result when the Negro in Africa is given an opportunity for self-development under more or less favorable conditions and with only helpful contact with the whites? Of the former condition, the United States accords of course the most illuminating example, while the free colony of Liberia gives the best answer to our second inquiry. These, together with the Negro republics of the Island of Haiti will prove the surest guides in our study of what can be made of the Negro and what he can make of himself under varying degrees of contact with the white race; therefore, before turning to our main subject of study, we will consider the Negro in Liberia and in Haiti.

On the west coast of Africa, just where the enormous back-head of the continent makes its turn upward, lies the little Republic of Liberia. Along this upward waterline of the head, it stretches for about five hundred miles, from the Ivory Coast to Sierra Leone, while its other boundary lines run irregularly into the interior, enclosing an area of 41,000 square miles.

In 1816, the American Colonization Society was organized for the purpose of establishing a home, in the land of their forefathers, for the American Negroes who had regained their freedom. Hence the name Liberia, which was given to the small area at first acquired from the natives and later much enlarged. Jehudi Ashmun, an American, is credited with the actual founding of the colony in 1823.

The first, and perhaps the only, motive of the Society was to fulfill what they regarded as their solemn duty to the freed Negroes, and to do this in a way which they thought ought to be most agreeable to the Negroes themselves. No thought, apparently, was given to the tribes who would be neighbors of the new colonists. In the many years since the founding of the little Republic, the population of American Negroes has reached only the small aggregate of from 14,000 to 15,000, living in coastal regions. Contrary to expectations in America (and very likely also in Liberia), of a spontaneous movement of Negroes to Liberia after their emancipation, less than 2,000 have availed themselves, since the Civil War, of the privilege of returning to the land of their fathers. The balance of the population is made up of some 40,000 natives—some of them Christians—upon or within reach of the coast, and at least a million more who possess the interior. The greater part of these last are still savages, a few are Christians, while many have embraced the Mohammedan religion.

It does not require a vivid imagination to picture the tragic condition of the earlier colonists as they arrived in the fatherland, and faced a wild country to be subdued, savage kinsmen who were their foes, a land without law, and a climate without kindness. These freed Negroes were, by training and experience, alien to the natives, and strangers to their fatherland. The story of those early years must be read elsewhere; but this merest hint cannot but call forth sympathy for the actors in the drama.

For twenty-five years the Colonization Society directed the colonial policies, until, in 1847, the colonists declared Liberia free and self-governing, and fashioned a government modelled after that of their native America. Since then, the Republic of Liberia has held its place among the nations of the world, and its unique position as the only State in Africa over which the Negro exercises authority. All the rest of the continent has been divided among the European nations.

Of the effort of the Church to supply this lonely colony with her ministrations, it is not our purpose to speak in detail. That has been done elsewhere. Our present object is to see what the Liberians themselves have accomplished with the assistance of the Church. We may therefore pass over, with very brief notice, the story of the Church in Liberia, until the time when she developed a Bishop of the Negro race.

In 1833, through the activities of Governor Hall and others, a parish was organized at Monrovia under the auspices of the American Episcopal Church whose interest in the well-being of the colony had early been enlisted. Two years later, Mr. James M. Thompson, a Negro layman who, as lay-reader, had been holding the flock together, accepted the appointment as missionary on the part of the Church in America. A small appropriation was made, and a school was built at Mount Vaughan and opened, in 1836, with five boys and two girls as the beginning of an educational work which has been a feature of supreme importance to the development of the Liberian Church and to the Republic. On Christmas Day of that year, the Rev. Thomas S. Savage, M. D., arrived from Connecticut, the first white missionary sent by our Church to a foreign field.

In 1837, the Rev. and Mrs. John Payne and the Rev. Lancelot B. Minor, of Virginia, arrived, followed by others in fairly quick succession. For fifteen years these devoted servants of our Lord, battling with an unhealthy tropical climate, labored to establish the faith of the Colonists and to spread the Gospel among the neighboring natives. In 1851, the Rev. John Payne was called home to be consecrated and sent back as "Bishop of Cape Palmas and Parts Adjacent"; and, until 1869, he skillfully guided the enterprises of the Church. It is probably true to say that nowhere and at no time since the first three centuries of the Christian Era, has there been so much of heroism, and of tragedy, bravely and quietly and naturally endured, as in this mission of Liberia during the period of eighteen years which Bishop Payne's Episcopate covered and in the thirteen preceding it. It is rightly called the "Period of Establishment," when, at the cost of quite one-fourth of the splendid lives devoted to the cause, the foundation of the now native Church was firmly laid both to resist every shock of heathen attack and to offer its strength to the superstructure of the native living Temple of God.

And the call upon faith and zeal, so peremptory in Bishop Payne's life, was echoed to the Church at home. The answer came in the persons of both white and Negro volunteers;

AMONG THEM, THE REV. ELI W. STOKES, AND THE REV. THOMAS A. PINCKNEY, BOTH OF THEM NEGRO PRIESTS.

THOUGH IT HAD BEEN THE CONSISTENT DREAM OF BISHOP PAYNE, AND HIS STEADY LABOR TO REALIZE IT, THAT LIBERIA SHOULD DEVELOP ITS OWN PASTORS,—THAT THE TREE SHOULD BEAR ITS OWN APPROPRIATE FRUIT,—IT WAS NOT UNTIL NEGRO VOLUNTEERS IN AMERICA CAME FORWARD THAT HE COULD DARE TO FEEL THAT THE TREE WAS READY FOR THE FRUIT-BEARING SO NEEDFUL TO ITS LIFE. IN 1853, THE STAFF OF NEGRO CLERGY WAS GREATLY STRENGTHENED BY THE COMING OF THE REV. ALEXANDER CRUMMELL, WHOSE FATHER WAS A NATIVE OF THE GOLD COAST. THE REPUBLIC SOON ESTABLISHED THE LIBERIAN COLLEGE, OF WHICH DR. CRUMMELL WAS A DISTINGUISHED PROFESSOR. THROUGHOUT ITS HISTORY, COLLEGE AND CHURCH HAVE BEEN CLOSELY ASSOCIATED IN DEVELOPING THE REPUBLIC. ALREADY, THROUGH THE SCHOOLS WHICH HAD GRADUALLY GROWN IN NUMBER AS IN ATTENDANCE, THE BOYS AND GIRLS HAD BEEN PREPARING TO TAKE THEIR PLACES IN THE COLLEGE, AND AS TEACHERS AND GUIDES AND PASTORS OF THEIR PEOPLE. THE COMING OF STOKES AND CRUMMELL AND PINCKNEY AND THEIR CHRISTIAN WIVES, FURNISHED MODELS IN RACIAL KIND TO BOTH BOYS AND GIRLS, THOUGH MRS. THOMPSON, WIDOW OF THE FIRST LAY-READER, HAD LONG BEEN A WHOLESOME EXAMPLE. SPEEDILY VOLUNTEERS OFFERED; AND, IN THE REPORT OF 1853, NEWS WAS SENT HOME OF THE ADMISSION OF TWO CANDIDATES FOR HOLY ORDERS FROM AMONG THE NATIVES—KU SIA, WHO, UPON BAPTISM, HAD RECEIVED THE NAME, CLEMENT F. JONES; AND MU SU, RENAMED JOHN MUSU MINOR. THESE MEN, ORDAINED ON EASTER, APRIL 16TH, 1853, WERE THE FIRST PRODUCTS OF THE LIBERIAN CHURCH SCHOOLS. FOLLOWING THESE ORDINATIONS, A STREAM OF NATIVE APPLICANTS, SMALL INDEED AS WAS NATURAL, FLOWED STEADILY INTO THE ORDAINED MINISTRY OF THE CHURCH.

BUT EVIDENTLY THE NEGRO COLONISTS OF LIBERIA HAD NOT YET PROVED THEIR ABILITY TO ORGANIZE AND MAINTAIN AN INDEPENDENT NATIVE CHURCH. THIS WAS NATURAL ENOUGH, FOR THE COLONISTS WERE POOR AND THE REPUBLIC ITSELF HAD NOT YET LEARNED HOW TO TURN ITS NATURAL RESOURCES TO PROFITABLE ACCOUNT. HENCE THE CHURCH IN LIBERIA HAD TO DEPEND ALMOST ENTIRELY ON FINANCIAL HELP FROM THE AMERICAN CHURCH.

IN 1855, THE BOARD OF MISSIONS IN NEW YORK, THROUGH ITS FOREIGN COMMITTEE, TOOK THE FOLLOWING ACTION, WHICH CHANGED THE ENTIRE STATUS OF THE WORK IN LIBERIA. "*RESOLVED*:

that the whole extent of the American Colonial Settlements in Western Africa, including the State of Liberia and the Colony of Cape Palmas, is considered as a missionary station occupied by this Committee." From this time on, the Mission of the Church was no longer the Cape Palmas Colony and its near neighborhood, but was co-terminous with the whole Province of Liberia.

This is, therefore, a good time to review the achievements of these most difficult years. *The Caralla Messenger*, the mission journal published in Cape Palmas, contains this interesting summary: "It is just 19 years, last Christmas Day, since the Rev. Dr. Savage formally opened the Mission at Mount Vaughan in the only building connected with it, and this but half finished. On that day, only about a half-dozen communicants, if so many, were connected with the Episcopal Church. Since then, 'through the good hand of our God upon us,' the Mission has established permanent stations, of greater or less efficiency, at fourteen different places, amongst colonists and natives. It has expended for churches, mission-houses, and school-houses, a sum not less than one hundred thousand dollars. In the day and boarding-schools sustained by it, not fewer than three thousand children and adults have received the rudiments of a Christian education. From six, the communicants—some of whom are now living, some dead—foreign, colonists and natives—have numbered at least three hundred. The number, at the present time, is two hundred and forty-one. The blessed Gospel is preached regularly to four colonist congregations, in some twenty different native tribes, and to one hundred thousand people. There are now, including the Orphan Asylum, seven commodious mission-houses, three churches completed and a fourth nearly so—two being of stone, one brick, and one wood—besides one very superior school-house and several more indifferent, for colonists and natives. A more sufficient cause of thankfulness still, is to be found in the number and character of the schools connected with the Mission. The High School and female day-school at Mount Vaughan; the Orphan Asylum at Harper; the native schools at Fishtown, Rocktown, Cape Palmas, Cavalla, Hening Station, Rockbookah, and Taboo; the boarding and colonist day-school at Bassa Cove, the Female High School at Monrovia, and the native boarding and colonist day-school at Clay-Ashland, give evidence of earnest and well directed effort to diffuse Christian instruction throughout the bounds of the Mission."

But this hopeful, almost buoyant, message was followed at the close of the next year, 1856, by great distresses, many deaths of faithful workers, war among the savage tribes, and hostilities between the Government and the natives, resulting in the loss of Mission property—all of which brought disaster, and retarded the work.

The years of the Civil War in America were especially trying, since revenues from the Mother Church were much decreased. Work had to be curtailed. Yet, through all the trials, the laborers in the field, missionaries, catechists and teachers, remained steadfast under the leadership of Bishop Payne who saw clearly that the hope of the Liberian Church lay in the gradual development of the will and ability to become self-supporting, and the arousing of missionary zeal toward the unevangelized tribes from the coast inland.

In 1862, the Bishop wrote, "We endeavor always to impress upon our native converts that the lesson God means to teach them, by the troubles in America, is to exert themselves for their own support and that of the Gospel in their midst. And they feel and acknowledge the situation."

In that year, the organization of the Church was strengthened, and the widely scattered missions brought into more compact oneness, by the formation of a General Missionary Convocation to bring the whole Church together in conference and mutual communion at stated times. A full account of this appears in *The Spirit of Missions* for August, 1862. Later in this year, Mr. Samuel D. Ferguson, a Negro colonist, was appointed Principal of the Mount Vaughan High School, and thus began his training for the later leadership of the Liberian Mission.

Before the close of the trying War period, the Mission sustained the loss of one of its oldest (in point of service) and one of its most efficient teachers, Mrs. Elizabeth M. Thompson, who, for twenty-eight years, taught in our Mission schools. She was a native of Connecticut, of Negro blood, born in 1807. In 1831, she emigrated to Liberia where she began work as a teacher in an infant-school in Monrovia. She later moved with her husband to Cape Palmas, and was associated with his work there and at Mount Vaughan, where, in 1833, he was appointed as lay-reader in charge of our budding work. Her husband died early, and she continued her work as teacher with great devotion until within a short time of her death, when ill-health obliged her to resign. She continued lighter labors in St. Mark's Hospital almost to the end, which came in April, 1864. Mrs. Thompson was an excellent Christian character, faithful and zealous and greatly beloved by all, an example to her race, and her death caused great sorrow in the entire community.

In 1871, after thirty-one years of devoted labor in foundation-building, Bishop Payne found himself obliged, by ill-health, to give up his work. Simply and modestly he gives the following account of his stewardship.

"To the praise of His grace, God has prospered the work of my hands as well as prolonged my days. At my own station (Cavalla) I have baptized 352 persons, of whom 187 were adults. In the Mission I have confirmed 643 persons. I have lived to ordain Deacons—two foreign, eight Liberians, four natives—in all, fourteen; of Presbyters, three foreign, seven Liberians, one Native—in all, eleven; or, altogether, twenty-five ordinations have been held. And at twenty-two places along 250 miles of what was, fifty years ago, a most barbarous heathen coast, has the Church been planted, and radiating points for the light of the Gospel established. Nine churches may be considered established and supplied with ministers of the Country. Besides schools, common and Sunday, we have a High School for boys, a Training School for young men, and an Orphan Asylum to take care of destitute children in the colonies. The Church and Mission by God's blessing, may be considered established."

Meanwhile, the Rev. Mr. Auer, the only white missionary left after the Bishop's withdrawal, had been even more busy than ever, with his American and native Negro co-workers, in building up the waste places and planning for the extension of work; in preparing native candidates for the Ministry, in which Mr. Crummell was chief factor; in building new and repairing old school-houses; and in recruiting the ranks of the white staff. The strain had been too great, and he lived for less than a year after his consecration as Bishop Payne's successor in the Episcopate. A few months later, Bishop Payne also died in his distant American home.

Thus the Mission was left with only recently recruited white helpers; but these, with the fine band of Negro clergy, catechists, and teachers, went steadily and faithfully forward. As Bishop Payne had so confidently declared, "The Mission may be considered established"; and so it was. For two years, with many misfortunes, but always in the confidence of hope, the work went forward until, in 1876, the Rev. Charles C. Penick, D. D., was elected Bishop of Cape Palmas and, on February 13th, 1877, was consecrated in Alexandria, Va. He arrived in his new field in October, and, two months later, returned this message to the Church at home, which sounds discouraging enough: "I find the American Mission confusion worse confounded. The work here has been so long without any head that the disorder is very, very great. Every building connected with the Mission is tumbling to pieces. I can put my foot through the rotten floor in the room where I now write, and it is one of the best in the house, and the house as good as any in the Mission. Books are all moulded and bug-eaten to worthlessness; furniture eaten to honeycomb; records like autumn leaves, only not so close together; no school system, no educational system; not the first move towards self-support; many changes and old questions to be settled, and not enough clergy to form a court."

I wonder if the Bishop, coming upon an era of more than usual confusion, was not tempted into a judgment upon the basis of standards at home among a people with ten centuries and more of steadily increasing stability of government and social order? I wonder if he had not forgotten that, since Bishop Auer served only an invalided Episcopate of a few short months, the Mission had really been headless for a period of quite eight years—from 1869 to Bishop Penick's arrival in 1877? What might not have happened in any Diocese in America, in far more favorable circumstances, had that Diocese been left without a head for such a period? And I am quite sure that something like this happened; for, two years later, the whole tone of the Bishop's report clearly indicates it, as he thanks God for the healing of divisions resulting from lack of Episcopal oversight, and for the bringing of good out of the evils incidental to the years of war, throughout which the Church had saved many from starvation, slavery and death. "More scholars than the schools can take are coming from heathen tribes," he wrote in substance, "and some are seeing the Christ and following him." In addition to other activities, Bishop Penick wisely introduced a department of farming, both for instruction and for profit; and the report in 1879 shows its steady advance under the direction of Mr. Christian Schmidt, a volunteer who came out with Bishop Penick from America and whose name suggests a well-trained German farmer. Out of this enterprise grew one or more agricultural schools, until eventually, into practically all the schools of the Mission, most helpful industrial features were introduced. Doubtless, all should have begun with industrial training, and the discipline of hand and eye should properly have led to the training of mind, and upward to that of soul. More properly all must go together, notably, with primitive folk, since each reacts upon the other.

In 1882 the Bishop's health failed, and he was forced to return to America; and, the next year, finding his hope to return groundless, he tendered his resignation to the Board. Bishop Penick's noteworthy contribution to the Church and people of Liberia consisted in the practical industries and the business system introduced just when these became possible of a fairly successful adoption. He was a spiritual power always, as preacher and pastor. The statistics, at the close of his Episcopate, are thus given: "Total average attendance in the churches, 1,063; number of communicants, 567; attendance at Day and Boarding Schools, 392; at Sunday Schools, 719. Total number of agents employed, including the Bishop, 8 presbyters, 5 deacons, and others engaged in the Mission staff, 57."

So closes, for the time being, the succession of Bishops of an alien race in Liberia. Against this time, God had been preparing a great Negro leader for His Church. After a trying vacancy of three years in the Liberian Episcopate, the Rev. Samuel D. Ferguson was elected, in 1884, and consecrated the following year.

Bishop Ferguson was the second Negro of our Episcopal Church to be consecrated as Bishop, the Rt. Rev. Dr. Holley of Haiti being the first. He was born in Charleston, S. C., on January 1st, 1842; and, while ill, was baptized by Bishop Gadsden at the request of his Roman Catholic mother. In 1848, the family moved to Liberia, where the father and two children soon fell victims to the tropical fever, leaving the mother and Samuel David to establish their home in the new land. Bishop Payne took charge of the boy, put him at school, and was as a father to him in his formative years and until he became, first a teacher, then a priest of the Church. While still a student, he was a Christian teacher to his less fortunate fellow students. From one post of responsibility to another his faithfulness and growth in grace and wisdom combined to call him. When Bishop Penick arrived, he quickly singled out Mr. Ferguson, in his business administration of the Mission, as a fit person to be the business agent of the Cape Palmas District. He was for many years the President of the Standing Committee. The fatality of the climate among the white missionaries, the growing emphasis put upon the aim of the Church to grow into a native national Church, the increasing growth in culture and in grace of the Negro clergy, had all conspired to arouse in the Liberian Church the desire for a Bishop of their own race, and in the home Church the willingness to grant it. In the Rev. Samuel David Ferguson, as the trial proved, the man was found eminently fitted for the sacred office and the arduous tasks. After his consecration in Grace Church, New York, the Bishop visited the home of his childhood, Charleston, and other points in the South. His first service as Bishop was in Norfolk, Va., where he confirmed a class for the Rev. J. H. M. Pollard in the Church of the Holy Innocents—a day of days for the Negro brethren of Norfolk and of America. Another such day was that on which he was received with glad, loving, enthusiastic welcome by his own people, the shepherd raised in his own fold—Liberia. All honor to the devoted white men who, in successive martyrdoms, gave their lives in devoted service to their black brethren; but is it either ungenerous or untrue to think, and to write the thought, that from earth and heaven must have come the glad acclaim to the black Bishop, blood of his people's blood and bone of their bone! "Thrice welcome to our Bishop, thrice honor to God that His grace has been sufficient for us!"

Bishop Ferguson, while on the voyage to America for his consecration mapped out his plans for development. Among the enterprises projected were a theological school of high grade, a medical college for whose conduct native physicians had been preparing, and an industrial school completing the design of his predecessors. Upon his return to Liberia, as Bishop, he was met by immediate and significant evidence of his people's gratitude for a Bishop of their own race. Before the year closed, the King of the Grebos presented himself to the

Bishop for baptism; and later, the King's wife, thus opening a wide door of future influence for the Church, though the habit of polygamy temporarily deterred many from surrender to the Faith which forbade it.

Most encouraging was the personal interest of the President and members of the Cabinet, and of the Mayor of the capital city and most of the officials. E. J. Barclay, Secretary of State, was Superintendent of Trinity Sunday School, and others were active on the vestry or as worshippers.

In 1888, after another journey to the United States, the Bishop set about establishing a Manual Labor Farm, for the founding of which Mr. R. Fulton Cutting of New York, had given $5,000, with a view to the instruction of boys in industries, and to serve as a pattern for other similar institutions. One hundred acres were bought, and the site was renamed Cuttington in honor of the founder. Thus was the Bishop enabled to begin one of the great enterprises to which he had set his efforts in his initial plans for development. An interesting sidelight is thrown on the success of these enterprises by the Rev. Mr. Fair in describing his work at Bassa. The coffee crop here was nearly doubled in one year through the use of improved methods, and the whole crop was sold to Park and Tilford of New York—a testimony to the excellence of the sample. Later reports of our Mission farms, though perhaps not so favorable, fully justified their establishment.

Another stimulating evidence of the new life in the Mission, is contained in the report of the year 1889: "The native converts are becoming increasingly interested in the spread of the Gospel and evincing a desire for self help"— such is the message. Church after church set itself the task of raising as much as possible for the support of the rector and the meeting of its home charges, while some also included contributions for the general work outside their borders. This marks the beginning of a new day for the Liberian Church, when the vision of a mission to others is dawning.

In 1890, a high recognition of the Negro leadership of the Church came in the election, by the authorities of the

REPUBLIC, OF THE REV. G. W. GIBSON AS PRESIDENT OF THE COLLEGE OF LIBERIA.

IT IS OFTEN STATED THAT THE NEGRO, LEFT TO HIMSELF, IS LIABLE TO MORAL DEGENERATION. IT IS INTERESTING, THEREFORE, TO NOTE THE HIGH STANDARD OF MORALS MAINTAINED IN THE LIBERIAN CHURCH UNDER BISHOP FERGUSON AS SHOWN BY THE FIRM DISCIPLINE WITH WHICH, ON THE RARE OCCASIONS WHEN IT PROVED NECESSARY, HE IMMEDIATELY ELIMINATED FROM THE ROLL OF WORKERS ANYONE WHO SHOWED DISREGARD OF CHRISTIAN STANDARDS OF MORALS.

AGAIN, WHILE THE MISSIONARY ZEAL OF THE LIBERIAN CHURCH WAS, TIME AND AGAIN, THWARTED BY HOSTILITIES AMONG THE TRIBES IN WHOSE BORDERS MISSION WORK WAS CARRIED ON, THERE IS ABUNDANT EVIDENCE THAT FOUNDATIONS WERE BEING LAID. THUS WHEN, IN 1892, THE TRIBES OF THE CAVALLA REGION WERE NOTIFIED BY THE BISHOP THAT DISTURBANCES CAUSED BY THEM NECESSITATED THE DISCONTINUANCE OF MISSION WORK, THE CHIEFS, WITH ONE ACCORD, BEGGED FOR A WITHDRAWAL OF THE NOTICE, AND THAT THEY BE NOT DENIED THE LIGHT OF CHRISTIANITY.

ONE OF THEM IS QUOTED: "WE ARE LOOKING TO YOU, AS THE PEOPLE THAT STARTED LEADING US TO THE GREAT ONE, STILL TO CONTINUE HIS MESSAGE AMONGST US. BUT IF YOU MEAN TO LEAVE US TO REMAIN IN DARKNESS, PLEASE LET US KNOW; FOR WE DO NOT THINK IT RIGHT TO SEEK IT ELSEWHERE UNTIL WE HEAR AND KNOW THE SAME FROM YOU, THAT YOU HAVE ALREADY GIVEN US UP. WE CLOSE WITH THE FOLLOWING—THAT WE SINCERELY AND EARNESTLY NEED THE PREACHING AND TEACHING OF THE WORD OF GOD AMONGST US WITH MORE FORCE AND SPIRIT THAN EVER IN OTHER PAST TIMES. WE ARE SINCERELY AND EARNESTLY YOURS FOR WHOM GOD'S SON DIED TOO.

SIGNED, TEBA YUE HUE, KING."

MANY A WHITE CHURCH MIGHT ENVY SUCH A WITNESS TO ITS LABORS.

IN THE YEAR 1895, THE EFFORTS OF THE CHURCH TOWARD SELF-HELP AND NATIONAL ENTITY HAD SO FAR PROGRESSED AS TO GIVE BIRTH TO A NEW ORGANIZATION—"THE BOARD OF DIRECTORS OF THE PROTESTANT EPISCOPAL CHURCH MISSIONARY SOCIETY OF LIBERIA, FOR THE CONDUCT OF THE BUSINESS OF GOD." THIS ORGANIZATION WAS EFFECTED BY THE GENERAL CONVOCATION OF THE CHURCH OF LIBERIA MEETING IN ST. MARK'S CHURCH, HARPER, AND HAS CONTINUED EVER SINCE WITH APPROPRIATE CHANGES IN NAME AND IN CONSTITUTION.

Steadily the native Church grew—the children of early converts in the ranks, still more of the grandchildren. From these, the ordained ministry is now being recruited, teachers prepared, doctors taught, nurses trained, Christian mothers and fathers raised up to be called blessed of their children. The general level of life is surely and steadily being raised. It has produced not a few worthy to be held in memory. Not the least among them, as earnest of what the race is capable of, was the Rev. M. P. Keda Valentine, who died on July 11th, 1896, and of whom Bishop Penick, his former Bishop, on hearing of his death, wrote: "He was one of the foremost spirits who ended the forty years' war between two factions of the Grebo tribe. He was foremost in Latin, Greek, Hebrew, music, athletics, courage, marksmanship, statesmanship, and Christian character amongst his fellows. Deeds of daring, self-sacrifice, patient endurance, forgiveness, and justness cluster about this man's life as about few I have ever seen or read of.... For six years I was in touch with Keda Valentine as his Bishop; I, coming from the center of Christian culture and light; he, from the depths of heathen corruption and superstition; yet I cannot recall one solitary instance when this man, by word or deed, fell below the mark of lofty Christian manhood as we know it. No duty assigned was ever too hard, no promotion over him ever drew a word or look of protest, no echo of envy did I ever hear from his lips. I saw him sit amongst the kings and sages of his people, where no other young man had ever sat, and when I asked them why he was there, they answered, 'True, he is very young, but God has put plenty of His Book in him, and he is fit to sit with us and make laws.' Now he is gone to join the other brave, cultured, true spirits—Montgomery and Walters—three bright stars in that dark land's firmament."

Bishop Ferguson died on August 2, 1916, just one hundred years after the organization of the American Colonization Society, to which the Liberian Republic owes its existence. The Rev. Mr. Matthews furnishes the statement here quoted which contains the facts about the District just prior to the Bishop's death: "When he was made Bishop, the Church had but ten clergy in the District; today we have 26, all colored. Then only 24 lay helpers; now we have 74. Then but 9 day-schools, with 284 pupils; now we have 25 schools with 1,094 pupils. From 5 boarding schools with 251 scholars, we have now grown to 20, with 596 boarders. The number of Sunday School scholars has increased over 2,000. The number of stations and churches has increased 150 per cent, and the communicant list has grown over 2,000. From being, in 1885, absolutely dependent for support on the Home Church, the Liberians, in 1913, contributed nearly $7,000 toward self-support."

We must not close the story of Bishop Ferguson's devoted labors without a reference to his relation to the Republic. This relation was unique. The Bishop grew to be the chief citizen, the "Grand Old Man" of the Republic. In his quite fifty years of service as teacher and Bishop, he had trained many of the rulers and legislators in whose hands the destiny of Liberia lay. These men knew him as man, as teacher, as Bishop. They knew his honor, his love for country and people, his wisdom, his unselfishness. They trusted him. He was their adviser. At crucial times he was called to address and to advise their Congress. The President felt that in him a wise counsellor was at hand, and he used him as the Bishop was willing to be used. Well did the Liberians say of him, with set purpose to abide by it: "Let us imitate the good example he has set us."

Yet still the Negro Church of Liberia, while proving itself capable of developing individual Christians of high character, did not seem prepared for full independence. Three years passed, during which time the matter of the Liberian Episcopate was discussed in all its bearings. There were strong arguments in favor of a Negro Bishop, possibly with a white Archdeacon as his adviser; but finally it was deemed best by General Convention to appoint a white Bishop, and at its meeting in Detroit in October, 1919, the Rev. Walter J. Overs, a man of long experience in Africa, was elected Bishop of Liberia. Consecrated two months later, he at once left to assume his new duties.

But the Liberian Church was not to be left without a native Episcopate. The Rev. T. Momolu Gardiner, a native of the Vai tribe, and a priest of high Christian character, had long since given evidence of what the Negro can attain to under the training of the Church. The Liberians themselves had expressed an eager desire for a Bishop of their own race, and no one was more fitted to fulfil those desires than Mr. Gardiner. In October, 1920, therefore, he was elected by the House of Bishops as Suffragan Bishop for Liberia, and was consecrated on June 23d of the following year.

Bishop Gardiner is a native, a fruit of St. John's School, and of the Divinity School at Cuttington. In his consecration sermon, Bishop Overs thus graphically pictures the task to which the new Bishop is called, and for which God had been preparing him: "You and I have travelled through much of Liberia together. You know the field and the work. You are a member of the Vai tribe, one of the most promising tribes of Liberia. But it is the only tribe of the Republic that is influenced by Mohammedanism. Your name is Momolu, which means in English Mohammed. Your father—a Mohammedan priest—gave you that name, but he also sent you to a Christian school, to learn letters. You learned to be a Christian. Gradually you have come to the position which you now hold. What a responsibility is yours! You must claim your tribe for Christ. Just before I left Monrovia, last month, one of your chiefs, a Mohammedan, came to me and said, 'The mosque in my town is falling down; if you will send me a teacher, I will build a Christian church and school in the very place where the mosque has stood.' It is prophetic. It will come. Then there are twenty other tribes in our District for whom little has been done from the standpoint of religion, education, or development in any way. You particularly represent these people. Your work will not be easy. Nothing worth while is. The work is vast. The task is tremendous. But the opportunity is magnificent."

Who can withhold his prayers of deepest sympathy for this David of his race, going forth against the mighty, new-clad in armor still being tried? Can we fail continually to hold close in our hearts the white Bishop and the black Bishop, as each sustaining the other and supplementing the lack of the other, they cross the borderland of the heathen and go forward with the Cross.

We are now in a position to reach some fair conclusion as to what the Negro is capable of when placed on his own feet in a more or less favorable environment. And let it be borne in mind that we are here dealing with a people of precisely the same stock as our own Negro population.

Apart from what we have considered in these pages, we may with confidence adduce the statements contained in the Report of the Commission to Liberia, sent out by the Church in 1918. This report is contained, in full, in the *Spirit of Missions* for June, 1918.

The Commission calls attention to the difficulties, both external and internal, which the Negro Republic has had to face from the very beginning. Powerful foreign nations on either side of her, though friendly towards her, have pre-empted much of her valuable territory for debts incurred, thus indicating what may yet befall. Poverty and lack of technical skill have prevented her from discovering and developing her own resources, while there has been no lack of those who would exploit her to their own selfish advantage. Unavoidable conditions, not inherent in the race, have made well-nigh impossible the establishment of an adequate school system, without which free institutions must always be in danger. The Government has had to face constant internal disturbances due to tribal warfare often stirred up by self-seeking individuals; hence, much of her strength, which should have gone to developing her resources, has been expended in preserving respect for law and order.

Yet the Commission found the Liberian people realizing clearly the obstacles to be overcome in self-development, and calmly and courageously facing problems which demand for their solution the most perfect skill, and earnestly endeavoring to overcome natural obstacles such as only wealth wisely used can control. "To think what would be the effect throughout the continent of Africa if, in Liberia, free institutions were definitely established, is to make one tingle with enthusiasm. Nor is there any question but that this is entirely within the ability of the people if they have the kind of help which only the Church can render. This can be freely given without fear of loss to Liberia and without resulting in dangerous dependence on her part."

A free and stable government has been established by the Liberians themselves, and it has stood the test of time and of innumerable obstacles measurably overcome. It is an honest government, Christian at heart and in ideals; but it lacks knowledge and skill and training to realize its ideals. It has no model to work by. The ability to bear responsibility is the difference between a free man and a man in bonds, and it is from this kind of bondage that the Liberian suffers because, with all the willingness in the world, he has not had the opportunity to make responsibility count. These things

EMPHASIZE THE ABILITY AND COURAGE AND INDUSTRY WITH WHICH THE REPUBLIC IS FACING THE OBSTACLES TO HER GROWTH.

THE COMMISSION REPORTS MOST HOPEFULLY CONCERNING THE STATE OF THE LIBERIAN CHURCH: "WITH OPPORTUNITY FOR EDUCATION SUCH AS WE, IN AMERICA, WOULD HESITATE TO CALL OPPORTUNITY, THE CHURCH HAS DEVELOPED A BODY OF CLERGY WHO NEED NOT BE APOLOGIZED FOR. WITH A TASK THAT IS LITERALLY COLOSSAL, THEY ARE WORKING AT IT WITH A GOOD WILL AND FULL OF HOPE. THE RELIGIOUS LIFE OF THE BODY OF THE PEOPLE IN THE CHURCH REMINDS ONE OF THE MANNER OF LIFE WHICH USED TO PREVAIL IN AMERICA BEFORE AMERICA BECAME RICH AND SOPHISTICATED. IN EVERY HOME WHERE WE HAVE BEEN, FAMILY PRAYERS HAVE BEEN A MATTER OF COURSE, AND THE REVERENCE WITH WHICH THE HOUSEHOLD HAS TAKEN PART HAS BEEN MOST REFRESHING. WHEN WE OFFERED THREE YOUNG GIRLS IN THE HOUSEHOLD OF THE CHIEF JUSTICE TICKETS TO A MOVING-PICTURE SHOW THEY THANKED US BUT DECLINED, SAYING THAT THEY WERE EXPECTING TO BE CONFIRMED THE FOLLOWING SUNDAY. ON ASH WEDNESDAY, FASTING WAS THE RULE—APPARENTLY A MATTER OF COURSE."

"THE HELP OF AMERICANS WILL BE NEEDED FOR THE ESTABLISHMENT OF THE CHURCH AMONG THE UNCIVILIZED. THIS IS NOT BECAUSE OF ANY LACK OF COURAGE OR INDUSTRY OR INITIATIVE OR DEVOTION ON THE PART OF THE LIBERIANS. WE SAW ALL THESE GRACES ABUNDANTLY MANIFESTED. BUT THESE PEOPLE ARE SHUT OFF FROM CONTACTS WHICH WOULD GIVE THEM THE EXPERIENCE AND KNOWLEDGE NECESSARY FOR AGGRESSIVE WORK. THEY KNOW WHAT THEY LACK, BUT MUST HAVE HELP TO FIND RELIEF." THE HELP WE RENDER MUST BE THAT WHICH WILL ENABLE THE CHURCH OF LIBERIA TO GET ALONG WITHOUT OUR HELP AND TO GIVE TO THE REPUBLIC THAT SERVICE BY WHICH THE REPUBLIC MAY BE ESTABLISHED.

"DURING THE PAST TWENTY-SIX YEARS, THE LIBERIANS HAVE HAD ENTIRE CONTROL OF THE CHURCH'S WORK, AND THE STRENGTH OF THE CHURCH HAS BEEN MULTIPLIED MANY TIMES. NO DAMAGE HAS RESULTED, AND NO WASTE OF HER MEAGRE FUNDS HAS OCCURRED."

"THE GLORY OF LIBERIA IS THAT IT IS A BLACK MAN'S COUNTRY—THE ONLY BLACK MAN'S COUNTRY ON THE FACE OF THE EARTH. THE INTERESTS OF HUMANITY, AS OF CHRISTIANITY, DEMAND THAT IT REMAIN SO. IN HIS PROVIDENCE, GOD SEEMS TO HAVE LAID UPON THE BLACK MAN THE TASK OF ESTABLISHING FREE INSTITUTIONS IN AFRICA. THE STORY OF LIBERIA'S EIGHTY YEARS IS AS THRILLING AS THAT OF

OUR FATHERS WHO, WE BELIEVE WERE SENT FOR A LIKE BENEFICENT PURPOSE TO THIS CONTINENT. THE FORTITUDE AND COURAGE AND PATIENCE AND ENTHUSIASM WITH WHICH THOSE PEOPLE HAVE DEVOTED THEMSELVES TO THEIR TASK, ARE BEYOND PRAISE. THE REPUBLIC OF LIBERIA, IN SPITE OF MALIGN INFLUENCE AND SLANDER AND MISREPRESENTATION, IN SPITE OF POVERTY WHICH WOULD HAVE BROKEN THE SPIRIT OF WHITE MEN, IS AN ESTABLISHED ENTITY. LET LIBERIA MAKE GOOD, AND SHE WILL HAVE MADE POSSIBLE THE REALIZATION OF THE PHRASE, 'AFRICA FOR THE AFRICANS.' THAT LIBERIA CAN DO IT, WOULD BE EVIDENT TO ANYONE WHO HAS THE WISH TO SEE AND COMPREHEND THE MIRACLE THAT HAS BEEN WROUGHT THERE."

Chapter III
THE NEGRO IN HAITI

The earliest instance of a State peopled and governed under a constitution made by Negroes, is the Republic of Haiti. For this reason it shares with Liberia a place of first interest among all the communities of the world. At its head is a president, with a parliament of two Chambers, acting under the revised Constitution of 1889. Republican in form, the spirit of the Government is French, since the language and customs are inherited from the French occupation of the island. Unfortunately, however, the country was, for years, ruled by a succession of military despots, each of whom was so occupied with maintaining his position against rivals that, even if capable of doing so, he had no time to develop the rich natural resources of the country or to establish democratic institutions. The population has, therefore remained a backward race.

The history of Haiti began with its discovery by Columbus in 1492. The aborigines were Indians, but these were enslaved, some sent to Europe, and the balance gradually exterminated. To take their places, negro slaves in great numbers were brought over by the Spaniards at first from Europe, later from Africa.

Columbus established six flourishing settlements, including the present capital; he opened mines, and established agriculture. Sugar was introduced, and ultimately became the chief crop. It is evident that, from the very outset, slave-labor was used in the development of this colony; and further, that the slaves employed in Haiti were brought thither from Europe. It may, therefore, be of interest to recall the facts concerning the first establishment of negro slavery in the Western Hemisphere. For this, we must turn back the pages of history to a period fifty years prior to the discoveries of Columbus.

In 1442, during the reign, in Portugal, of King Henry, surnamed "The Navigator," Antam Gonsalvez, returning to Portugal from an African cruise, brought with him three captive Moors. The Moors offered to purchase their liberty with negro slaves if their captors would return them to Africa. Prince Henry accepted the offer, giving a reason which served to quiet his own conscience, while suggesting a subtle motive which was to justify the traffic for many a long year to come. It was "because the Negroes might be converted to the Faith, which could not be managed with the Moors." So the trade was made—ten Negroes for three Moors—to the greater triumph of "the Faith." They were landed in Portugal in 1442; and, within two years, so zealous became the apostles of the Faith that the "Company of Lagos" was chartered, others soon following, whose industry included the traffic in slaves from Africa. Hundreds, yearly, were brought into Spain and Portugal.

Alfred H. Stone of Dunleith, Mississippi, furnishes the facts which we are using, and from which we quote rather freely:

"In the description of the landing of the first Negroes—— we may read the first count in the indictment against modern slavery, destined to be repeated ten thousand times in the English-speaking world during the 417 years which elapsed between that time and the destruction of slavery in the Southern States: 'But now, for the increase of their grief (*Chronicle of Azurara*), came those who had the charge of the distribution, and they began to put them apart, one from the other, in order to equalize the portions; wherefore it was necessary to part children from parents, husbands and wives, and brethren from each other. Neither in the partition of friends and relations was any law kept, only each fell where the lot took him.' We are further informed that the Infante was present to look after the fifth part, which fell to his share, 'considering with great delight the salvation of those souls which before were lost.'"

In 1501, nine years after the discovery of America, the first slaves were transferred from Spain to the King's Colony of Haiti. At first, only Negroes Christianized by European life, were sent. This custom probably persisted until the direct trade between the colonies and Africa was begun, in 1518. It was then that the good Roman Priest, Las Casas, desiring to save the Indians from the killing labors of the mines, advised the direct traffic in slaves with Africa. Without impugning Las Casas' motives, it is only fair to add that, in the estimate of the time, one Negro was equal to about five Indians in mining-labor. This great value of negro slavery as an economic institution is, above all considerations, responsible for the enormously increasing traffic from this date down to the era of abolition. Such, in brief, is the story of the institution of slavery in our hemisphere, and especially in Haiti.

Because of the insular life, the great predominance of the Negroes, the almost constant civil strife, and the slight contact of the races, the conditions for the maintenance of racial traits and habits were more favorable in Haiti than anywhere else in America; hence the development and persistence of that debasing mixture of magic, superstition, and secret rites, known as *Voodoo*, which seems to permeate all classes of the Haitien population. The Roman Church, by law established in the Republic of Haiti since 1869, seems to have failed in eradicating this cult or of reaching helpfully any large proportion of the people. This is doubtless due in part to the difficulties of travel in the interior, and to the fact that the evils of illiteracy were never sufficiently realized to compel any adequate attempt toward education. The children of the wealthier, city-bred people have usually been sent to France to school; the great mass of poorer children entirely neglected. Inherent laziness served to re-enforce the ill effects of ignorance among the people at large, and instability of Government added a further counter-weight against progress.

Again, the laws of marriage (or the lack of them) have had a vicious effect upon the Haitien Negro. Where marriage is not recognized by the State as legally necessary to the legitimacy of children and is therefore rarely observed, polygamy with all its debasing results is bound to lower the moral tone of a people, and of the Negro above all. It is fair to say that, after a century of independence and self-government prior to American intervention, the people of Haiti, kindly and hospitable and amenable to civilizing influences as they are, gave little, if any, evidence of progress.

The proverbs of a people, just as their folksongs, reveal much as to the character, habits and mental traits. The *Spirit of Missions* for September, 1875, records a collection of Haitien Proverbs, from which these are selected:

It is only the knife that knows the heart of the yam—used with various meanings—as, for example, distrust outward appearances, it is not what you see that counts, and the like.

Shoes alone know if the stockings have holes—doubtless a later application of an older proverb, meaning that only the most intimate know the weakness of others.

Conspiracy (or combination) *is stronger than witchcraft*—a useful encouragement for minds just emerging from superstitious fear into the conviction that "spirits fear a crowd."

The wild goat is not cunning that eats at the foot of the mountain—a comment on the folly of ignoring points of vantage, and of abandoning safety for publicity.

If the frog says that the alligator has sore eyes, believe him—the trustworthy testimony of an unfriendly neighbor.

The ox never says to the pasture, "Thank you"—a possible implication that it is only a beast which gives no thanks for favors.

Joke freely with the monkey but don't play with his tail—an evident warning against outraging the sensitive feelings of others.

All wood is wood, but mapou (a worthless wood) *is not cedar*, meaning that all people are good for something, but none good for everything.

There are certain qualities of mind and character which appear plainly in these popular sayings, and the latter are re-enforced by an old Southern proverb of doubtful origin which applies to the Haitien, as to our Southern Negro, however lowly. "If you burn him for a fool, you will lose your ashes." Certainly it is a huge mistake to discount the Negroes' wisdom, no matter how homely and often rude the expression of it.

We may now return to a consideration of the history of the island, pausing only to call attention to the fact that we are chiefly concerned with the western third composing the Republic of Haiti. For here, in contrast to the Dominican Republic, with its largely mulatto population under the political domination of whites, we find a population, ninety per cent of which is pure Negro and with a Negro government.

We shall here see the Negro developing out of slavery in an insular, French colonial environment.

In 1630, a mixed company of English and French occupied the Island of Tortuga and became formidable buccaneers. Obtaining a foothold on the mainland of Haiti, their descendants became French subjects when, by the Treaty of Ryswick, in 1697, the part of the Island which they occupied was ceded to France. A period of strife followed, involving the whites, the mixed, and the Negroes. As a result, the whole Island became subject to France. In 1801, Toussaint L'Ouverture, a Negro of remarkable military genius, successfully renounced the authority of France and set up the Republic of Haiti with himself as Governor. Captured by treachery, he was taken to France where he died in prison in 1803. The next year, Dessalines became Governor, massacred the remaining whites, proclaimed himself Emperor, and was assassinated in 1806. The Spaniards again reappeared about this time, and gained a footing in the eastern part of the Island, but, after years of cruel warfare, they failed to maintain their hold, and the Negro Republic of Santo Domingo was established in 1844. More recent events are newspaper history, read and fairly known by all.

The Island is shared by the two Republics, the western third being Haitien, the eastern two-thirds Dominican. The former is French in language, the latter Spanish. Repudiation of obligations and a continuous state of disorder finally compelled the American Government to intervene. In 1915, a concordat was established with the Government of Haiti whereby American resident officials were given certain advisory powers, and in 1916, the Dominican Republic was taken in charge by an American Army of Occupation. Thus the United States became a virtual protector and guardian of the peace, serving the whole Island in an educational and developmental capacity, very much as in the Philippine Islands.

The political history of the Island of Haiti, whether in its French or its Spanish aspect, naturally led to the early establishment there of the Roman Catholic Church, and in 1869, it became the representative of the established religion of the Haitien Republic. In this Faith the people were brought up (in so far as they came under any Christian teaching at all). Thus, from the beginning, the history of the Church in Haiti differs widely from that in Liberia.

In 1861, an American negro priest—the Rev. James Theodore Holly—went to Haiti with a company of 110 persons, and there formed the nucleus of a Mission of the American Episcopal Church.

The early history of this leader of his people is full of interest as is shown by the following, taken from *Men of Maryland* by the Rev. Dr. Bragg of Baltimore, the historiographer of his race in the Church.

Born in Maryland, in 1829, young Holly was baptized by a Roman Catholic priest from Haiti who had fled to this country before the fury of the Negroes, at that time intent upon ridding their country of the last vestige of the white people. Twelve years later, he was confirmed by the Archbishop of Baltimore, the Rt. Rev. Dr. Eccleston, but his connection with the Roman Church was not destined to be permanent. He learned the trade of shoemaking, working in Washington, and later in Detroit. Influenced probably by the peculiar circumstances of his Baptism, and by the romance of the Negro Republic battling for self-government, he seems early to have been possessed with the desire to offer himself as a helper. This he disclosed in a letter written, after his desire had been gratified, from his Haitien home: "I was ordained deacon in 1855 (by Bishop McCoskry of Michigan) with the express understanding that I should be sent to work in this field. As a matter of fact, two weeks after my ordination, I set out from Michigan to New York, from which I was sent ten days later, by the Foreign Committee of the Church, to collect information as to the possibility of establishing such a Mission, and returned from thence with a favorable report. Six years were then spent in gaining pastoral experience for the work in view; and to this end I was advanced to the priesthood by the Bishop of Connecticut on the 2nd of January, 1856, when I accepted the pastoral charge of St. Luke's Church, New Haven, in that Diocese. Aside from the active pastoral work of that congregation, every fitting occasion was seized during those six years to stir up an interest by tongue, pen, and the press, in the contemplated Mission. In 1861, my face was again set towards Haiti, accompanied by 110 persons (of whom I was the pastor) for the practical establishment of the Mission in this land."

Among the most forward in promoting this enterprise, were the Bishops of Ohio and Connecticut. It was through the latter's influence, that his Diocese generously aided the Mission of Mr. Holly for sixteen months. At the close of 1862, the Mission in Haiti was adopted by the American Church Missionary Society, with Bishop Lee, of Delaware, as Provisional Bishop. The next year, the Bishop made his first visitation to the new Mission. From this time forward, the Church at home kept a kindly oversight over the Mission in Haiti. So faithfully and successfully did Mr. Holly and his band of Churchmen work, that, in 1871, the Haitien Church, by vote of its Convocation, petitioned General Convention to elect and consecrate a Bishop for Haiti. The response was sympathetic, and the petition was referred to the Board of Missions to ascertain the best means of securing adequate Episcopal supervision. Three years passed, and the Convention of 1874 entered into a covenant between the Protestant Episcopal Church in the United States and "The Orthodox Apostolic Church" of Haiti. The following are the more important terms of this covenant: (1) That the Church in America recognizes the Church in Haiti as of right and of fact a foreign Church under the definition of our Constitution; and that, with this recognition, the assurance is given that the Church in Haiti will enjoy the nursing care of the Church at home until such care shall no longer be needed. (2) That the Church will designate and consecrate one of the Haitien clergy to be Bishop of Haiti. (3) That a Commission of four American Bishops will be named to act with the Bishop of Haiti as a Board of Administration, to extend the Episcopate when needed, and to administer discipline pertaining to the Episcopal order. (4) That the Church in Haiti agrees to guard, in all their essentials, a conformity to the doctrines, worship and discipline of the Protestant Episcopal Church in the United States, departing from them only as local circumstances require. (5) That the Haitien Church agrees to concede to the Church at home the designation and consecration of the Bishops of the Church in Haiti until three Bishops shall have been established therein.

In accordance with this agreement, General Convention, in 1874, elected, from among the clergy of Haiti, the Rev. James Theodore Holly, and, on Nov. 8th, in Grace Church, New York, he was consecrated as Bishop.

Eager to be back at work, Bishop Holly set sail ten days later, and thus describes the glad, joyous reception of his people upon his arrival at his home and old parish, Port-au-Prince: "I found all the members of my family and of Holy Trinity on the lookout for me. A deputation of the clergy and of the vestry were in waiting with a carriage. I was conducted to the church where the faithful had gathered for a thanksgiving service, entering under the triumphal arch surmounted by the phrase, 'Gloria in excelsis Deo,' which had hastily been constructed that morning, after the steamer had been seen at a distance entering the harbor. The service over in church, I retired to my residence, where I was besieged during the rest of the day by visits of the members of the congregation, from neighbors, friends, and the citizens in general, all coming to welcome me home, and to present me their warm congratulations. These visits were continued in like manner all the next day. Saturday morning I called on the President of the Republic, and the Minister of Public Worship, to pay my respects, and thus rendered to the civil authorities the honor due to them before appearing to officiate in public in my new vocation. Mr. Preston, the Minister Plenipotentiary to Haiti, had made an official report to the Government of my consecration as Bishop, at which he assisted in Grace Church, New York, and the President and Minister expressed to me their highest gratification at the new position thus gained by our Church in Haiti. Advent Sunday, I addressed the English congregation after Morning Prayer at six o'clock, and the French congregation at the 9 o'clock service, taking, on each occasion, for my text, those words of Zechariah iv. 6, 'Not by might, nor by power, but by my Spirit, saith the Lord of hosts.' The drift of my remarks, in setting forth all the circumstances leading to and attending my consecration to the Haitien Episcopate, was to impress on the minds of the people committed to my charge that human instruments and worldly powers were of no value in this matter, but that the movements of God's Holy Spirit were the basis of all our successes in the past as they must be of our hope in the future."

Thus began the Episcopate of the first negro Bishop of the American Church, a man of unusual ability; of highly developed powers of leadership; a courteous, Christian gentleman.

The statistics for 1875 are: The Bishop; priests, 6; deacons, 4; lay-readers, 14; candidates for Orders, 3; number of missions,

18; of churches, 3; of rectories, 2; whole number of souls, 751; of communicants, 238, and perhaps 3 schools.

The Bishop's early letters supply information concerning the nature of the field. Transportation was difficult with only paths or trails to guide the traveler. All of the travel by land was done on horseback, and the Bishop was gradually accumulating the means of locomotion. On December 24, 1874, he writes, "I have already bought a mountain saddle (to be paid for when convenient to me) and have yet to get bridle and knapsack. However I borrow these things, with the use of a horse, to make my trip tomorrow"—a comfortable, leisurely approach to equipment, with the blessing of handy friends by the way.

Other travel was by boat, very leisurely too, a week to come and go if the places be near, and more if they be far. The Bishop is already longing for a "Bishop's Horse," and says so; a "Bishop's Boat" is probably as yet only a dream, because "the interior stations are among the most interesting in which we are engaged, and work ought to be encouraged and strengthened by the visits, as often as possible, of the missionary-in-chief."

The Bishop's travels were wonderfully fruitful—large classes confirmed, and glad response given to the ministrations of their new, but already beloved, Father in God. The schools, too, were filled with boys and girls in training for the new day of the Church in their homeland. But church-buildings were lacking, and many of the congregations were worshipping in rented or private houses.

In Port-au-Prince, the capital, the Church was firmly established and included two parishes where services were constantly held in English as well as in French; but the poverty of the people was a drawback to independence. The Bishop writes, "We have from three to four hundred souls to look after in this way at the Haitien Capital; but the most of them are in unfortunate or very moderate circumstances, and therefore can do but little to sustain the Gospel among themselves. They must not be expected to keep up, without generous aid from abroad, the work of the Gospel in Haiti. The time may come when the great mass of men of the so-called better classes, who now live in complete religious indifference, shall be awakened to a sense of their great spiritual danger. Here, as elsewhere since the beginning, it is the common people who follow Him gladly."

For their shepherding, the Bishop felt the need of more men from the American Church, consecrated to the Master's Mission. There were men already at his disposal, but the means to employ them were lacking. Here again, as so consistently in our mission-fields, because of the poor, cramped purse, the Bishop—sent to organize and to evangelize—was estopped within hearing of yearning calls for preachers and teachers. "I need to found at once a Theological Training School for young men desirous of preparing themselves for the Ministry, and a first class Female Boarding School," the latter, to supply his schools with teachers. How like the cry of Ferguson in Liberia is this urgent appeal of Holly in Haiti, and how natural the cry of each!

By the close of the first year of the Bishop's episcopate, he had completed the round of visitations of his rather disconnected group of missions. The year had been a very successful one, yet not without its distresses and difficulties. There had been 106 confirmed, 36 baptised, and schools well filled with children. Property had been repaired, and at least one church-lot donated for the new parish of St. Andre, in Trianon. This was given by General Hyacinth Michel, who was appointed lay-reader of the new parish.

We have lingered about the opening scenes of the Bishop's first year that we might gain an insight into his plans and methods, and realize something of his difficulties and successes.

During the early years, the Bishop is evidently intent upon the great purpose which consistently faced him—the creating of a national Haitien Church. After five years, his report to General Convention in 1880, tells us how earnestly he has been striving, more to strengthen the faith and character of the little parishes, than to extend faster than such faith and character can be established. The statistics show but a feeble increase in the numerical strength. "Nevertheless," writes the Bishop, "there has been, during this period, that which figures cannot show, viz., an increase among its numbers of the knowledge of the ways of the Church, greater attachment to the same, and a decided deepening of their inner spiritual life. Our Church in Haiti also occupies the high vantage-ground of being the only denomination exercising independent local jurisdiction and aspiring to a complete national organization. In pursuance of this object, this feeble Church has now twice as many native ordained clergymen as all the other religious bodies combined. It has also more advanced stations than any of them, established in the interior country districts among the rural population, where the heathen customs of Africa have hitherto prevailed. Our work has conquered the esteem and respect of the Government and people of Haiti, and enjoys the full protection of the authorities under the guaranties of the Constitution and laws of the country."

It is probably because of this conservative and cautious policy of Church extension, and still more because of the poverty of the people and the small amount available for clerical salaries, that we find no appreciable increase in the number of clergy and other workers. For the Bishop, in 1883, reiterates the statement, "We have no difficulty in finding the needed laborers; not only can we find them among ourselves in Haiti, but, in case of need, the whole of the British West Indies are at our beck and call, islands where the Church and Church training institutions have long been established. Therefore the only difficult problem that remains to be solved is that of supplying the money necessary to inaugurate the central training institution that we propose to establish." Such an institution, it will be remembered the Bishop had had in mind from the very beginning.

Passing rapidly over the intervening years to 1895, the story reminds one of the more tragic record of the foundation-period in Liberia. There were successive angry waves of warfare, involving the Church through her people and property; and the sometimes surly, sometimes lethargic, aspects of peace, which in turn follow family outbreaks. There were rebellions against the ruling powers; and frequent changes among the officials upon whose stable protection the Bishop, in earlier years, had grounded so much of his hope. There were the severe losses of people, and the death of pastors and teachers, bringing burdens upon the Bishop's aging shoulders. But through it, he battled bravely onward, filling the ranks as the communicants fell away, and slowly, very slowly adding to them; supplying the leaders as these passed on, and very slowly increasing their number.

In 1891 *The Twenty-fifth Convocation of the Haitien Church* (being the seventeenth of the Bishop's episcopate) organized itself into a Missionary Society, of which each member of the Church was declared a member. The Convocation itself became the Board, while the Bishop and other officers formed the Executive Committee. The churches were growing in the spirit of self-help. The people of a mountain section, poor in worldly goods, earned the money for, and built the walls of, their church; and the President of the Republic gave $650 to supply the roof. The church at Port-au-Prince, destroyed some years before and hindered in its plans for rebuilding by various obstacles, was settled in a better location through the good offices of the President and Parliament. These are samples of the problems, some perplexing, still others stubborn, which delayed and harassed the workers. A year of peace (and there were not many) witnessed "some steps taken in advance for the further extension of our Gospel work. Three new stations (in 1890) for the preaching of the life-giving Word have been occupied." One of these was initiated by a small band in the mountain region, who, gathered into the Church and knowing the blessing, desired to spread the Gospel to their unconverted neighbors.

In 1891 the Bishop records, with pride, the fact that one of his presbyters, the Rev. Shadrach Kerr, had been transferred to the Diocese of Florida. Mr. Kerr, while still canonically attached to Haiti, had been temporarily at work on the Isthmus of Panama, under Archbishop Nuttall of Jamaica. Another of the Haitien clergy had been transferred to Jamaica. Thus the products of the Church in Haiti were being spread abroad.

A farm-school for education and demonstration, established about 1887, and requiring three years of instruction for graduation, sent out its first class in 1890. One of the young men at once established a school in a needy mountain district. Thus was demonstrated the quality of these negro Churchmen.

The year brought much sickness, however; and amongst the victims was the young teacher, who had already begun the work of a missionary to his people. It was doubtless this visitation which constituted a call to the Bishop to hasten the establishment of a Medical Mission, so greatly needed, and which had already been his earnest wish. Two students had been sent to Boston, to be trained, one as a physician, and the other as a pharmacist. The Bishop sent an urgent appeal for sufficient money to establish these men in their professions upon their approaching graduation.

The year 1892—the fourth centenary of the discovery of America—was a memorable one in the annals of their history. "Here," wrote the Bishop, "the first permanent settlement of Europeans in the New World was made. Here, later on, the first landing of African slaves in this hemisphere was effected. Here, following the example of the United States, the second colonial yoke of European vassalage was broken, and the second free and independent nation of the New World thereby established."

"This people," continues the Bishop, "by the powers of the merely natural man, have indeed conquered their earthly freedom, but they still have need to obtain the emancipation of the soul—freedom from sin—by that liberty wherewith Christ only can make us free."

The plea of the Bishop rings out—his plea for help to realize his well-founded plan which again and again he had described to the Board of Missions, and which follows the eloquent and urgent presentation of the claims of Haiti just quoted.

"For upward of thirty years, since it was planted here in 1861, we have stoutly held on to the almost forlorn hope of making this Church a blessing to the people among whom our lot is cast. Among other things for which we labor, we are striving to complete the well-being of their acquired nationality by raising up a native clergy among the people, bone of their bone and flesh of their flesh—a most desirable object, the accomplishment of which no other religious denomination, aside from ours, has essayed to realize in a systematic manner. To this end, we need a theological training-school. We are also wrestling with the problem of extending popular education among the illiterate masses; to do which, more successfully, a better equipped normal school is needed. We also have in hand for solution, the problem of introducing scientific medical treatment of the sick and neglected poor; to do this effectually, we need a well-organized medical mission. We have the personnel (doubtless the two students referred to above) for such a mission, but we need the pecuniary means necessary to effect such an organization."

Surely this plan should have found friends and helpers in America, and must find them even yet, in order that Haiti may realize a more worthy measure of the ideal of her first devoted Bishop. He closes his report thus: "On our part, we ask you brethren, one and all, to pray for us that our faith fail not, and that we may not grow weary in well doing, but be always animated with the blessed and soul-consoling hope, that in due season we shall reap, if we faint not." In 1895, after seven years of weary but persistent patience, the Bishop was able to hold services in the church at Port-au-Prince, the center of the mission work of the District, which was so far completed as to be fit for occupancy. The same year he was able to announce the joyful tidings that "five of the sons of our clergy have been graduated as physicians to co-operate with the clergy in the work of the Gospel among the afflicted poor; and thereby emphasis has been given to the humane aspect of the Gospel of Christ, while the ministry of the clergy gives due emphasis to its divine aspect. We have every reason to believe that our triple Gospel work, carried on by ministers, physicians and teachers, has given us a grasp on the very vitals of the nation, which will grow with its growth, and increase with its strength."

But the Bishop is not deceived by the fresh hope which the year has brought. "Let it be borne in mind," he writes, "that our work is carried on under the enervating influence of the Tropics, and amidst the sluggishness of an undeveloped people; and, therefore, such marvels of rapid progress are not to be looked for here as characterize the railroad speed with which things more forward in the United States under far more favorable circumstances."

During the next ten years, the first steps were taken towards the realization of the most important features of the plans for the District. In 1901, following Bishop Holly's visit to the States, the much needed Theological School was opened at Port-au-Prince, with the Rev. P. E. Jones as Dean, and the Revs. Alexander Battiste and Theodore F. Holly as professors. Dean Jones had, for many years, been the very efficient Principal of one of the Schools of the Republic at Aquin, and his experience and success had singled him out as the man to reorganize the Lancastrian School, needing reconstruction, in the capital city. His transfer by the Government made it possible for the Bishop to realize at least the beginnings of the Theological School, so long a cherished hope. At first this school was conducted in the evenings, after the example of the Government Law School. Six students were enrolled at once, and others awaited the means necessary for expenses. This school, or its successor, has been reopened by The Rev. A. R. Llwyd, and three new clergymen recently graduated.

The Medical Mission, so important to the development of the Bishop's plans, began to take definite form about 1904, through the training of two nurses in an institution extemporized for that purpose by Dr. A. C. C. Holly, a son of the Bishop. In 1905 two lots were secured for the projected hospital and dispensary, for the erection of which funds were asked of friends in the States. Awaiting these, Dr. Holly opened a small hospital in one of the mission-buildings, with Miss Lidia Boisson, one of the nurses trained locally, in charge of the sick ward. Two other young women had been sent to the United States for training as nurses, at the expense of the Board of Missions. The ministrations of the hospital and the ministries of the physicians and nurses wrought untold blessings to a country to which sanitation was unknown and hygiene unheard of. The well-laid plans of the Bishop and his co-workers, the physicians, were never completed; for, with the coming of the Americans, in 1915, all sanitary and medical work was taken over by them, and the necessarily imperfect equipment and methods of the old medical mission were thereby superseded.

In the face of the infirmities of greatly advanced age, Bishop Holly continued to administer the difficult work of the District until March 1911, when he was called to his rest. Through fifty years of devoted, unfaltering service he gave himself to the land of his adoption, and the people whom he loved. In 1855, he had sought the permission of our American Episcopal Church to found the Church in Haiti. In 1861, the petition granted, he landed with a colony of American Negroes in Haiti. During the succeeding years he raised up a

NATIVE MINISTRY—A NOTABLE ACHIEVEMENT IN VIEW OF THE FACT THAT THE ROMAN CHURCH, WITH A FAR LONGER HISTORY OF MISSIONARY WORK IN HAITI, HAS, TO THIS DAY, NOT A SINGLE NATIVE PRIEST THERE. DURING THE FIRST YEARS, SERVICES IN THE CAPITAL WERE SAID IN BOTH FRENCH AND ENGLISH; AT THE CLOSE OF THE BISHOP'S EPISCOPATE, THERE WERE BUT FIVE ENGLISH-SPEAKING COMMUNICANTS RECORDED.

WHEN THE REV. MR. HOLLY ARRIVED IN 1861, HAITI, EXCEPT FOR A FEW CHURCH MEMBERS IN THE NEW COLONY, WAS BARREN GROUND FOR THE CHURCH. IN 1874 THE BISHOP AND HIS STAFF OF SIX PRIESTS AND FOUR DEACONS WERE MINISTERING TO NEARLY ONE THOUSAND SOULS, OF WHOM 238 WERE COMMUNICANTS, DIVIDED AMONG 18 MISSIONS.

AT THE CLOSE OF BISHOP HOLLY'S ADMINISTRATION, THERE WERE 12 PRIESTS; 2 DEACONS; 2 CANDIDATES; 2 POSTULANTS; 18 LAY-READERS; 54 TEACHERS (OF WHOM 9 WERE IN DAY-SCHOOLS); AND 26 MISSIONS. MORE THAN 2,000 SOULS WERE UNDER THE MINISTRATIONS OF CLERGY AND TEACHERS, WITH 651 COMMUNICANTS.

THE NATIONAL CONVOCATION OF THE HAITIEN CHURCH, FOLLOWING THE BISHOP'S DEATH, REQUESTED THE CHURCH IN AMERICA TO SEND A DELEGATION TO HAITI TO LOOK OVER THE FIELD AND COUNSEL WITH THE NATIVE CHURCH AS TO THE MEASURES TO BE ADOPTED WHICH WOULD BEST SERVE ITS INTERESTS. MEANWHILE, THE REV. PIERRE E. JONES, DEAN OF THE CONVOCATION, ADMINISTERED THE DISTRICT PENDING THE DECISION OF OUR AMERICAN CHURCH. MR. JONES GIVES THE FOLLOWING MOST SIGNIFICANT INFORMATION: "ONLY A STRONGLY ORGANIZED, NATIONAL, PROTESTANT EPISCOPAL CHURCH CAN SURELY BRING ABOUT A REVOLUTION IN THE RELIGIOUS VIEWS AND OPINIONS OF OUR ROMAN CATHOLIC FELLOW-CITIZENS. THE ENGLISH WESLEYANS ENTERED HAITI IN 1818, AND HAVE TODAY FOUR MISSIONS, TWO NATIVE MINISTERS AND ONE FOREIGN. THE AMERICAN METHODISTS ENTERED THE FIELD IN 1824, AND HAVE TODAY ONE MISSION AND ONE FOREIGN MINISTER. THE AMERICAN BAPTISTS ENTERED THE FIELD IN 1848, AND HAVE TODAY THREE NATIVE MINISTERS AND THREE MISSIONS. THE PROTESTANT EPISCOPAL CHURCH ENTERED THE FIELD IN 1861; IT BECAME AN AUTONOMOUS CHURCH IN 1874; AND HAS TODAY FIFTEEN WELL-ORGANIZED PARISHES, SEVEN MISSION STATIONS, AND FIFTEEN ORDAINED NATIVE MINISTERS. WE HAVE ALSO A YOUNG HAITIEN IN THE DIVINITY SCHOOL IN PHILADELPHIA, AND A YOUNG WOMAN IN THE DEACONESS HOUSE IN THE SAME CITY. AFTER THEIR COURSES ARE COMPLETED, THEY WILL RETURN HOME TO STRENGTHEN OUR LITTLE ARMY OF BRAVE ONES."

In January, 1912, the Board of Missions requested the Rt. Rev. Dr. Knight, Bishop of Cuba, to be the chairman of the delegation in response to the above request. The Bishop, with his party, arrived at Port-au-Prince about the close of the month, and later sent an interesting account of the expedition, which was published in *The Spirit of Missions* for September and October 1912. As a sidelight on the difficulties which had beset the path of Bishop Holly, this extract from Bishop Knight's letter is illuminating. Referring to Port-au-Prince he says, "There is a saying that it has been burned and rebuilt every seven years as a result of frequent revolutions." And then, as an earnest, let us devoutly hope, of what may come to pass, this sketch is given of the newly elected President Le Conte. "It was some time before I understood that this gentle and soft-spoken Negro was the Chief Executive of this turbulent Black Republic. There was nothing uncouth about him; he had no braggadocio manners; on the contrary, he seemed refined and effeminate. It was hard to realize that only a few months before he had landed on his native shores, after five years of exile; had gathered a few followers; and had swept his course onward to the Capital, until the martial Simon fled before him. With his advent to power, better days for Haiti seem to have dawned. Le Conte belongs to one of the oldest and most refined families of the Island. He is grandson of the first President, the military genius who, taking up the sword of Toussaint, completed the deliverance of Haiti from France. He has been highly educated, and has spent much time abroad. He has come to power when militarism has ridden his country for many years, and crushed out its industries. He is reversing these things. The number (of the army) has been reduced. The new broom is sweeping clean. Our Church can be a great aid at this time if she rises to the opportunity."

Bishop Knight met and advised with the Council of the Haitien Church, called in special session. The action taken is thus described: "The Convocation remained in session for a week; and, finally, by a practically unanimous vote, passed a resolution requesting the American Church to receive the Haitien Church as a Missionary District." One can but regret, and deeply, that the purpose of Bishop Holly's fifty years of vision, which seemed so great to him, should have been abandoned, when the Convocation voted to relinquish its autonomy. Let us hope that this is but a temporary status.

It was not until 1913 that General Convention could reply to the request of the Church in Haiti, and meantime Bishop Knight was deputed to render Episcopal service there. In that year General Convention, having elected the Rev. Charles B. Colmore as Bishop of Porto Rico, appointed him to the charge of the Missionary District of Haiti. The connection between Porto Rico and Haiti is exceedingly remote, and the means of transportation most difficult, so that Bishop Colmore found a task impossible to be done efficiently. Like a good soldier, he obeyed orders, and the Church must take all the onus for the short-comings. He holds the District together, promoting the existing enterprises, and greatly encouraging the work of the Woman's Auxiliary, of which little or no notice seems previously to have been taken. To overcome, as far as possible, the disadvantages of the conditions, the Rev. A. R. Llwyd was appointed Commissary to the Bishop, and, in 1918, he began work in this capacity. With headquarters in Port-au-Prince, Mr. Llwyd has indefatigably labored to repair rents and build up waste places.

The reports, as well as the comments of visitors, all agree that what is most needed for the upbuilding of the people is the Christian Industrial School. This was Bishop Holly's dream; it must still be the objective until realized.

In 1919, General Convention resolved that Haiti must have a Negro Bishop of its own, and elected the Rev. Samuel Grice of Payne Divinity School. He felt constrained to decline, and the Rt. Rev. Dr. Morris, of the Panama Canal Zone, was appointed to take the oversight of the Church in Haiti. At best, an absentee Episcopate can do little more than conserve, and Haiti awaits the day when love and generosity shall overflow in the American Church, so that she may fully seize the day of opportunity. It is her chance to do for the struggling Church of the Haitiens what our American representatives, civil and military, are doing for their Government,—settle and establish and train, and thus in good time set free a people from the thraldom of ignorance and vice. It is doubtful if either can succeed without the other; it is pretty certain that social training must fail unless religious culture accompany it. "Except the Lord build the house, their labor is but lost that build it."

Chapter IV
THE SLAVE AND THE FREEDMAN IN AMERICA

The importation of Negroes to the American mainland began about 1525, following the license for such traffic by Philip of Spain. From that time, through Spanish and French companies chiefly; and after the Spanish Armada, through English companies chiefly, the trade in African slaves was vigorously pursued. While statistics are unreliable, Stone approves the guess that "the number transported to Spanish America may be said to have been somewhere between four and seven millions; for English America, insular and continental, about three millions during the century preceding the Revolution. The number brought into the Thirteen Colonies may have been about three hundred thousand."

The first slaves (about twenty in number) were brought to our colonies by a Dutch vessel which landed at Portsmouth, Va., in 1619, just twelve years after the first permanent settlement by the English. This we have upon the authority of John Rolfe. Thus the Negroes, though not of their own wills, were among the first settlers of the new country. It is vain to discuss the question of responsibility, or of moral culpability. However revolting to the modern mind and heart, slavery was the inheritance of our forefathers, practiced in every conceivable form, not only in Africa, but among every people and in every land. When practiced within racial lines, it extended all the way from the kindly, household slave relations of the Romans, where slaves were sometimes the teachers of their masters' children, to the relations with war-trophies to be sold or exploited as chattels. When practiced inter-racially, the differences of race were apt to harden into prejudice with its general indifference to the consequences of cruelty. But in either case, it was the universal practice of heathen and Christian peoples until a comparatively recent time. Moral culpability did not enter into the reckoning of the ages preceding ours, and responsibility was readily admitted or never questioned. And this was true of our colonist forefathers who carried on the slave traffic as sellers and buyers in the early days. Even

After the consciousness of the wrong of it had been awakened in many by the experiences of slavery, they found themselves the victims of a system of social life which they would gladly have escaped. This is equally true of the Southern and the Northern colonists.

It was because of the rapid growth of this consciousness of the wrong of slavery, naturally quickened by the advance of Democracy during the eighteenth century, that the traffic was made illegal in 1807. It was also because so large and so respectable a number of slave-holders realized themselves to be the victims of an inherited system of social life from which they could find no satisfactory means of escape, that the system took more and more the form of humane feudalism in which, however, the vassals were workers and not soldiers to be protected and not exposed to danger. And when Emancipation came, there were not a few who felt and expressed it. "It is not the Negroes who are emancipated, but the Whites; only we cannot realize it until the last of our old people are gone." And this was true, for the Negro had yet to learn the art of freedom and acquire its character before it could become the reality as well as the blessing it should be. True, too, that the white man was not yet emancipated, for he had still to fulfil the obligation to his old people, many of them children as yet in development, loving and beloved; and this, in many cases, he did to the last dollar and to the last dust of meal, and to the last old servant laid to rest.

No one, except perhaps the political economist here or there, or some fond soul of the olden time who has been asleep ever since, will attempt to defend slavery; yet it is also difficult to understand the philosopher, North or South, White or Negro who attaches nothing but obloquy to it, and sees nothing that is good resulting from it. Doctor Murphy's opening chapter of *The Basis of Ascendency* begins with this true assertion: "It is so frequently assumed that the most significant factor in the history of our Negro population is the factor of its exploitation, that a word of contradiction is never quite out of place. Within its actual environment, whether North or South, this population has suffered much, but it has received more." And emphasizing the inevitable co-partnership of the two races in the task of progress which the White alone has been responsible for forming, he adds: "It (the Negro population) has become involved so inextricably in the fate of a far more efficient social group, that the conditions of progress within this stronger group have become the conditions which must surround and advance the life and fortunes of the weaker."

Dr. Booker T. Washington is never an apologist for Negro slavery, but he recognizes a large fact when he sees, side by side with "the great curse (of slavery) to both races," this evident shaping of its ends. "God, for two hundred and fifty years, in my opinion, prepared the way for the redemption of the Negro through industrial development." It is the story of this redemption that must now occupy our interest.

Our first chapter sought to draw the picture of the Negro in Africa. We then saw him as he has developed under conditions of more or less segregation and self-government. Now we are to trace his development under American conditions, described by visiting students of slavery as the most kindly and humane ever experienced in such relations. Thus the Englishman, Welby, wrote in 1820: "After traveling through three Slave States, I am obliged to go back to the *theory* to raise any abhorrence of it. Not once during the journey did I witness an instance of cruel treatment, nor could I discover anything to excite commiseration in the faces or gait of the people of color. They walk, talk, and appear, at least, as independent as their masters; in animal spirits they have greatly the advantage."

Again, Basil Hall wrote, in 1828: "I have no wish, God knows! to defend slavery in the abstract; ... but ... nothing during my recent journey gave me more satisfaction than the conclusion to which I was gradually brought that the planters of the Southern States of America, generally speaking, have a sincere desire to manage their estates with the least possible severity. I do not say that undue severity is nowhere exercised; but the discipline taken upon the average, as far as I could learn, is not more strict than is necessary for the maintenance of a proper degree of authority, without which the whole framework of society in that quarter would be blown to atoms."

Human nature is much the same the world over, and this display of kindly humanitarianism, so noticeable to the traveling students, was probably but the outgrowth of the

EARLY CONDITIONS OF COLONIAL LIFE. THE SETTLERS IN A NEW LAND WERE BESET WITH THE PROBLEM OF LABOR TO DEVELOP THE NEW HOMESTEADS. ENGLISH FREEMEN WOULD RARELY ENGAGE THEMSELVES FOR SUCH WAGES AS EMPLOYERS COULD AFFORD TO PAY. WHAT MORE NATURAL THAN THAT THE LABORERS IN ENGLAND, WILLING AND OFTEN ANXIOUS TO EMIGRATE TO THE NEW LAND, SHOULD SELL THEMSELVES FOR A PERIOD OF LABOR SUFFICIENT TO PAY PASSAGE, INCLUDING A MEAGRE WAGE WHILE THE SERVITUDE LASTED. THUS INDENTURED SERVITUDE FOR THE COLONIES TOOK THE PLACE OF THE OLD SYSTEM OF APPRENTICESHIP SO LONG IN USE IN THE OLD COUNTRY.

WHEN NEGRO SLAVES CAME IN INCREASING NUMBERS, THE FORMER RELATION WITH INDENTURED SERVANTS MUST CERTAINLY HAVE ENTERED, MORE OR LESS, INTO THE INTERPRETATION OF THE RELATIONS OF PERMANENT SERVITUDE. ADD TO THIS THAT ALL ALIKE WERE SURROUNDED WITH THE POSSIBLE, AND OFTEN AROUSED ENMITY OF THE RED MEN, AND WITH A CONSTANT PERIL OF LIFE, WE HAVE FACTORS WHICH MUST GREATLY HAVE STRENGTHENED AND SOFTENED THE BOND BETWEEN WHITE AND NEGRO. IN THESE AND IN MANY OTHER CONDITIONS OF THE EARLIER DAYS OF THE SETTLEMENTS, ONE SEES THE CONDITIONS OUT OF WHICH KINDLINESS AND AFFECTION WERE WELL-NIGH CERTAIN TO GROW, AND THE WELL-RECOGNIZED MUTUAL PARTNERSHIP OF INTERESTS TO DEVELOP.

AND THIS IS JUST WHAT ACTUALLY HAPPENED FOR THE MOST PART. THE GROWING SENSE OF THE MUTUAL INTEREST AND DEPENDENCE, AND RESPONSIBILITY CONSTANTLY TENDED TO DEVELOP A RELATIONSHIP SIMILAR TO THAT OF THE OLD PATRIARCHATE. THE CONSTANT BATTLE WITH THE PRIMEVAL FOREST AND UNDEVELOPED NEW LANDS—A BATTLE TO BE WAGED SUCCESSFULLY ONLY BY THE IMPORTATION OF LABORERS, UNTAUGHT AND UNDISCIPLINED—CONSTANTLY TENDED ALSO TO DEVELOP THE RELATION OF THE TEACHER AND THE TAUGHT IN THE LARGER SCHOOL OF NATURE. SO THE SYSTEM GREW INTO THE FAMILY AND THE TRADE SCHOOL.

LET US DISMISS, WITH ONE PARAGRAPH, THAT OTHER UNSIGHTLY, OFTEN CRUEL, ALWAYS CONDEMNABLE SIDE OF SLAVERY—THE UNFEELING, RUTHLESSLY SELFISH AND CONTEMPTIBLE BUSINESS OF THE SLAVE-TRADER, WHO SOUGHT ONLY TO FILL HIS PURSE WITH GOLD THROUGH THE SALE OF "HUMAN CATTLE"—THAT UNSPEAKABLY LOATHSOME ESTIMATE OF THE NEGRO AS AN ANIMAL WHOSE RELATIONSHIPS WERE IGNORED, WHOSE LOVE WAS RIDICULED, WHOSE SENSIBILITIES WERE DESPISED AND WHOSE RIGHTS (FOR THE RIGHTS WERE THERE, EVEN THOUGH THE RIGHTS OF A SLAVE) WERE DENIED.

Slavery did, in some instances, present that aspect; but no one can read the story without knowing that that side was the horrid incident, and not the characteristic of the old feudal and patriarchal life. It was that feature which often hindered the development, upon the best lines, of the rude Negroes brought from Africa. It could not, however, stop it. Our purpose being to trace this development, we are led into pleasanter fields; for it is in the inner life of the White-Black family and school, that the story of the culture of the wild graft is written.

Professor Phillips, in his *American Negro Slavery*, tells us that during the first half century after the introduction of slaves there were comparatively few Negroes in the colony—Virginia—which received the first importations. "They had," he writes, "by far the best opportunity which any of their race had been given in America, to learn the white man's ways and to adjust the lines of their bondage into as pleasant places as might be. Their importation was, for the time, on but an experimental scale, and even their legal status was, during the early decades, indefinite."

There was, as yet, neither law nor custom establishing slavery as an institution. In fact it was custom that established the status of permanent servitude, while the laws only recognized it in defining the difference between the white indentured servant and the negro purchased slave. This did not become a subject of legal enactment until 1662. Prior to that time, Negroes were described as servants: "A few as servants for terms of years; some were conceded, property rights of a sort incompatible with the institution of slavery as elaborated in later times. Some of the blacks were liberated by the courts, as having served the terms fixed by their indentures or by the custom of the country." How much of trouble and distress would have been saved had the forefathers developed their slave problems after this precedent, rather than after that of their Spanish and English neighbors of the South Atlantic Islands!

Some of the Negroes had become landowners by the middle of the century, and some were themselves slave owners. More and more, however, the owners of Negroes were holding them tenaciously, and regarding them as salable property; and from, 1680 onward, the laws for slave control became as definite as those in the Islands.

The charter and later settlement of the South Carolina Colony, in 1663, by Sir John Colleton of Barbadoes and his company, for the purpose of attracting colonists from the English Islands, fixed the general legal status of slavery upon the American Colonies. This was made the more sure because in the first-settled coast regions of the colony, rice, and later indigo, were introduced as the staple crops, for the cultivation of which only Negroes could endure the necessary swampy conditions. The owners, dwelling in the neighboring pine elevations by night and in summer, went to their plantations only in the day time and in the winter season.

Likewise, in the Northern Colonies, without exception, the system found its way; first, through the enslaving of captive Indians, then, by 1630, of Negroes also. While the traffic in slaves persisted for a long time with Newport as the chief center, neither climatic nor economic conditions were favorable to the system. In one way or another, slavery declined, and the field presents little that is valuable to our study.

The Revolutionary War, with the Declaration of Independence, and its assertion of the freedom and equality of men as its justifying principle and motive, produced a profound effect upon the mind of America; not, indeed, sufficiently great to enable any State to enact laws looking to gradual emancipation, but great enough to arouse most of the Northern States and all of the Southern, except Georgia, to prohibit, by the year 1787, the further importation of slaves from beyond their borders. The Federal Congress was still, however, inhibited for twenty years, from enacting such laws.

The action of the State tended to stabilize social life, by reducing the number of strange Negroes from across the ocean; and to strengthen the ties of masters and servants, by prolonged association. The result was well-nigh universal in the Slave States in spite of South Carolina's repeal of its law, four years before the Federal Act was passed at the close of 1807. Meanwhile the introduction of cotton, in about 1790 as the chief crop of these States, proved to be the greatest material factor in determining the social and industrial life of the Eastern and Southern States, especially the latter. Once firmly established, following Whitney's invention of the cotton gin in 1793, it almost as firmly established the life of the Negro in his agricultural home.

The Louisiana Purchase, in 1803, and the expansion of sugar-planting on a large scale, completed, for many generations, the cycle of Southern agricultural industry. Since then, much has happened; but agriculturally the Negro's home is practically unchanged and his development has been through a stable school of arts which ministered to his rural life.

The pupils, we must bear in mind, came from many tribes of Africans. Professor John McCrady, in the course of a lecture to his students in Sewanee, said that he had clearly defined fourteen different dialects spoken by the Negroes of the Sea Islands of South Carolina, and did not doubt but that many more could be found by the student of the Southern Negro. Not only were the dialects different, but quite marked were the physical and mental characteristics. It is a mistake to imagine that all Negroes are alike. The pupils of the plantation school came to be known and rated personally just as the pupils of any school must be; and so, too, the children of the large patriarchal family.

The character of the plantation school was determined, partly by the crops raised, partly by the nature of the land, partly by the personality of the master and his foreman, partly by the number of workers, and partly by the neighborhood customs. Some neighborhoods operated on the gang system, dividing the workers into groups; others on the task system, allotting so much as the labor of the day; while still others used successfully both systems, often the former for men, the latter for women and younger learners.

If the owner had but one or half a dozen families of servants he usually labored with them at plough, or hoe, or wagon. If a greater number, his time was fully occupied in planning the work, and overseeing the workers. If the plantations were very large, the organization was elaborate and complete. In every case, to the Negro, as he came new from his African home and for long after, the school was most valuable and every day brought lessons to body, mind and soul. As the great majority of the old servants were congregated on the larger plantations, it was there that most of the training was received. Should the reader have access to one of a number of books like *A Southern Planter*, by Mrs. S. D. Smedes, the reading will be most delightful and not less instructive in its exact picture of the old régime. Or if a visit could be paid to Alfred Holt Stone's Dunleith Plantation (a very fine sample of many like it) in Washington County, Mississippi, there would be seen a perfect likeness of the old life, under the much improved conditions (in many respects) of free labor. For all that was best in the old régime, the mutual interest, the personal attachments, the mutual confidence, the pride in home, the loyalty and friendship between master and servant, has been preserved in the descendants of both. The statement just made and that which follows have been tested all over the South, and never found wanting whenever the two races are still found in the old homes. There never has been a place or time when there were more Christian Whites and Christian Negroes more earnestly interested in forming and keeping the highest and best race-relations, and in seeking the best interests of both races alike, than in the South at this present time. Unfortunately, they are not all Christians who call the name of Christ.

The organization of a large plantation had to be very perfect if it was to succeed in maintaining its great family. Phillips' *American Slavery* presents many samples and, with minute detail, describes the routine, interesting but not necessary to our study. One type will sufficiently illustrate the educative value of all.

The division into crafts was essential where the plantation represented a community well-nigh completely self-sustaining. There was the agricultural department, so ordered as to provide the right proportion of plowmen and hoe-hands, each with its foreman. In every case the foreman or head-man was a Negro of marked ability as a workman and leader, who was not a mere driver but a teacher. Generally he exacted the task and demanded that it be well done. Often he got what he wanted by tactful resource and consummate human wisdom, as one of them expressed it, "I never discouraged, but him that was hindmost I praised the most." His leadership involved every detail, both of prompt and well-done service, and of the care of the tools; in the case of the plowman, the proper care of the livestock and its management. There were the carpenter shops, where all the wood-work was done; with the house carpenter, sometimes the cabinetmaker, and always the toolmaker for the wood-work of plows, wagons, etc. Often, in the beginning, they had been taught by white experts fresh from their apprenticeships in England or Ireland. They understood the care and seasoning of timbers and lumber, from the cutting in the forest to the sawing and shaping in the shop. Under them there were often one or more young apprentices who had shown aptitude. The system, the exactness, the careful planning that no want should be unsupplied when needed; the care to be ready for instant repairs that other departments might not be delayed—all of this was entrusted to the head of each department of carpentry, who was a man to be trusted and relied upon; and the master, with mind always busy looking forward and eyes seeing everything, knew it, as in kindly confidential contact, he rather suggested and counselled than ordered. Here is a little extract from a colloquy once heard in a very busy time.

"Uncle Ned, where are those plow stocks? Didn't I tell you we would need them tomorrow"?

"Marse John, who is making dese plows? Don't I know when dey is needed"?

And with a chuckle, Marse John receives the retort of offended dignity, and beats a retreat, having seen the various parts of the plows, stacked in order, ready to be assembled in a trifle of time, and proud of the old reliable.

There was the blacksmith's shop, where everything was made, from a nail to a lock and key, from a plow-shovel to a wagon-axle and spindle, from a bridle-pit to steel stirrups. Gradually these were replaced by manufactured articles; but to the last, any might be repaired or replaced if necessity required.

The women had their tasks. There were the hoe-hands—women, boys, and girls—to be taught under easy, short tasks, but with the care always required by their foreman. There was the weave-room, where cotton and wool were spun and woven into cloth for home use. The dyeing was done at home. There was the sewing-room where, under the oversight of the mistress, clothing in proper quantity was cut and made for "top and bottom" wear. There was the day nursery where the young mothers, busied with the half tasks allotted them, left their little ones under the care of the older experienced women who, under the mistress, were at times nurses, and at other times mid-wives.

Some plantations also had "the sick house" for severe cases; but, in most cases, the sick were at home, visited regularly by master or mistress or both, and by the family doctor where his attention was needed. The last was often distant, and the master and mistress were generally good substitutes, always supplied with simple remedies. The day-nursery provided the opportunity for instruction in baby-farming, which many a mistress used to great advantage. For instruction in domestic service, the "Big House" was the school, and none better. A southern negro boy would as soon have been disrespectful to his father as "sassed" the dignified butler; a punishment would even more certainly have followed the latter, if known. And the relation of love between children and "Mammy," and between family and servants, is too charmingly commonplace to remark.

Dr. Washington, writing of God's hand in it all, says: "First, He made the southern white man do business with the Negro for 250 years in a way that no one else has done business with him. If a southern white man wanted a house or a bridge built, he consulted a negro mechanic about the plan and the actual building of the house or bridge. If he wanted a suit of clothes or a pair of shoes made, it was to the negro tailor or shoemaker that he talked. Secondly, every large plantation in the South was, in a limited way, an industrial school. On these plantations, there were scores of young colored men and women who were constantly being trained, not only as common farmers, but as carpenters, blacksmiths, wheelwrights, plasterers, brickmasons, engineers, bridge-builders, cooks, dress-makers, housekeepers, etc. I would be the last to apologize for the curse of slavery; but I am simply stating facts. This training was crude and was given for selfish purposes; and did not answer the highest needs, because there was the absence of brain-training in connection with that of the hand."

It is good to have the Negro speak for himself. The last sentence would have been written differently by his white friend. Though given for selfish purposes *in part*, the training was definitely also for the good of the pupil; and while often crude, it was more often very definitely expert. Some of the more skilled workers, in every generation of the slavery days and in spite of adverse laws, were taught to read and cipher; they drew their plans, estimated their materials, and made their own calculations for the work in hand. Yet it is also true that the laws against school-training, though never fully obeyed, vastly hindered the general development of the race.

One other important division of farm economics should be mentioned, i. e., the food supply, involving the raising of cattle, hogs and poultry; the cure of meats; the storage of grain and vegetables, etc. In all this there were plantation experts, as well as happy joyous faces and overfed bodies at "hog-killin' times." In practically all cases, Saturday was half-holiday, often utilized by the slaves in their home-gardens or in other work yielding money to be spent at their own pleasure. Poultry and eggs, the weaving of baskets or other articles, were other sources of income. Not infrequently the Negroes continued the crafts native to their tribes in Africa.

The houses of the servants, while far beyond those left behind in the "Dark Continent," and comfortable for the most part, were certainly not the sort in which a high moral life could be taught. Consisting often of only two rooms, sometimes three, the problem of sleeping-quarters in them seemed a secondary consideration. And while few planters of the olden days would admit less than a real interest in the morals of their servants, practically none provided the means of safeguarding them properly in the homes furnished. Yet it must be said that these quarters were generally better than those which the Negroes have provided for themselves "since freedom."

We turn now to the old plantation as the patriarchal family, with its valuable educative features in moral training and home-making. "The Big House" was the name given by the Negroes to the master's home, whether a log house or a stately mansion. The servants' quarters on the large plantation were often in the form of a village, with its streets, one or many, as the inhabitants required. Each house had its garden, its "hen-house," and generally its pig-sty; with its fruit trees, serving both for shade and for food. Other features of the village, the day nursery, etc.—have been mentioned. The system of life was co-operative. With the exception of the garden truck, the supplies came from the plantation storehouses and the flocks and herds. Fish from

THE NEARBY STREAMS, WILD GAME, AND NATIVE FRUITS OF FIELD AND FOREST, FURNISHED ADDITIONAL FOOD FOR ALL ALIKE.

"THE LIVES OF WHITES AND BLACKS," AS PROFESSOR PHILLIPS WRITES, "WERE PARTLY SEGREGATE, PARTLY INTERTWINED. IF ANY SPECIAL LINKS WERE NEEDED, THE CHILDREN SUPPLIED THEM. THE WHITE ONES, HARDLY KNOWING THEIR MOTHERS FROM THEIR 'MAMMIES' OR THEIR UNCLES BY BLOOD FROM THEIR 'UNCLES' BY COURTESY, HAD THE FREEDOM OF THE KITCHEN AND THE CABINS; AND THE BLACK ONES WERE THEIR PLAYMATES IN THE SHADED, SUNNY YARD, THE LIVELONG DAY. TOGETHER THEY WERE REGALED WITH FOLKLORE IN THE QUARTERS; WITH THE BIBLE AND FAIRY STORIES IN THE "BIG HOUSE"; WITH PASTRY IN THE KITCHEN; WITH GRAPES AT THE *SCUPPERNONG* VINEYARD; WITH MELONS AT THE SPRING-HOUSE; AND WITH PEACHES IN THE ORCHARD. THE HALF-GROWN BOYS WERE LIKEWISE AS UNDISCRIMINATING AMONG THEMSELVES AS THE DOGS WITH WHICH THEY CHASED RABBITS BY DAY AND 'POSSUMS BY NIGHT. INDEED, WHEN THE FORK IN THE ROAD OF LIFE WAS REACHED, THE WHITE YOUTHS FOUND SOMETHING TO ENVY IN THE FREEDOM OF THEIR FELLOWS' FEET FROM THE CRAMPING WEIGHT OF SHOES, AND THE FREEDOM OF THEIR MINDS FROM THE RESTRAINTS OF SCHOOL. WITH THE APPROACH OF MATURITY, CAME ROUTINE AND RESPONSIBILITY FOR THE WHITES; ROUTINE ALONE FOR THE GENERALITY OF THE BLACKS. SOME OF THE MALES OF EACH RACE GREW INTO RUFFIANS, OTHERS INTO GENTLEMEN IN THE LITERAL SENSE; SOME OF THE FEMALES INTO VIRAGOES, OTHERS INTO GENTLEWOMEN; BUT MOST OF BOTH RACES AND SEXES MERELY BECAME PLAIN, WHOLESOME FOLK OF A SOMEWHAT DISTINCTIVE PLANTATION TYPE.

IN AMUSEMENTS THERE WAS THE SAME MINGLING AND SEPARATION. NEVER A FOX-HUNT OR A RABBIT-CHASE, BUT SOME BELL-VOICED NEGROES WERE ON HAND TO "WHOOP-UP THE DOGS," AND, WITH CANNY KNOWLEDGE OF THE HABITS OF WILD THINGS, TO GUIDE THE HUNTERS, DOGS AND HUMANS, TO LIKELY LAIRS. SOMETHING LIKE THIS WAS TRUE OF EVERY OUTDOOR SPORT. IF THE NEGROES GAVE A DANCE, THE WHITE WERE THERE TO LOOK ON AND APPLAUD. IF THERE WAS A FESTIVITY AT THE "BIG HOUSE," THERE WERE SURE TO BE SOME FAVORITES FROM THE QUARTERS TO SEE AND HELP. WHO, THAT HAS HEARD THEM, CAN EVER FORGET THE IMPROMPTU CONCERTS SWELLING UP FROM THE QUARTERS ON MOONLIGHT NIGHTS? STARTING OFTEN WITH A SINGLE VOICE FROM THE STOOP OF A CABIN, AND TRAVELING FROM HOUSE TO HOUSE, UNTIL THE COMBINED VOICES SWELLED UPWARD AND OUTWARD AS A GREAT, EXQUISITE ORGAN FILLING ALL space—it was, in very truth, a human organ of God's fashioning. The memory brings melody.

Every step by the way was development from the savagery, often cannibalism, of African inheritance, to the awakening kindliness due to others, and the reverence for life as such. There were quarreling and fighting to be prevented or stopped. Punishment was often inflicted for such outbreaks. In some cases, the masters resorted to athletics as both a training in self-control and a means of working off surplus energy. Wrestling, boxing, racing and the like were practiced under the eye of the master, who acted as judge of the contest, and knew how to teach the contestants to compose ruffled feelings. Whether at work or at play, the old system was a school of training, under average conditions worth while; under the best conditions most valuable.

Some of the tribes of Africa had already developed agriculture to a degree. The American life immeasurably improved both method and purpose. And what a wholly new conception of family and social life was born in them! Polygamy had been too universally fashionable in the old land to admit the ties of family. No fondling there of little ones, no rejoicing in the growing lives; only the interest in the chattel, to be sold if the child be a girl, if a boy, all ties gone with the mother's dried breast.

But, in the new life, love, long starved, re-awakened in tremendous force. High human emotions were developed, released and expanded under ever increasing kindly relations, growing more and more into affectionate attachment which was tried by shot and shell, by hunger and thirst, and not found wanting. This a South Carolinian wrote in 1852, a few years before the testing time of war: "Experience and observation fully satisfy me that the first law of slavery is that of kindness from master to slave. With that ... slavery becomes a family relation, next, in its attachments, to that of parent and child." The Negro did not write that—not many could—; but nearly all learned to live it.

Conditions differing from those of the Negro in slavery existed, even during the period of slavery, among a constantly growing number of free Negroes who formed a distinct class both North and South. While a very few free Negroes came into the colonies from the islands, and, in the early period, a larger number at the expiration of the indentured service, this class was formed either by the purchase of themselves by the Negroes, or through their manumission by generous or grateful masters. Typical of the first, is "the deed signed by Robert Daniell of South Carolina, in 1759, granting freedom to his slave, David Wilson, in consideration of his faithful service, and of £600 currency in hand paid." Illustrative of the second, is "the will of Thomas Stanford of New Jersey, in 1722, directing that, upon the death of the testator's wife, his Negro man should have his freedom if, in the opinion of three neighbors named, he had behaved well."

It is to be noted, too, that the democratic philosophy of the Revolutionary period, inevitably and immediately producing the abolition movement, stimulated very greatly private manumissions throughout the colonies, which persisted, in spite of reaction, to the very end of slavery. Thus Philip Graham, of Maryland, made a deed in 1787, by which his slaves were converted into servants for terms, and in which he recited, as the reason, his conviction that "the holding of his fellowmen in bondage and slavery is repugnant to the golden law of God and the inalienable right of mankind, as well as to every principle of the late glorious revolution which has taken place in America." About the same time, Richard Randolph, of the Roanoke family, wrote to his guardian, "With regard to the division of the estate, I want only to say that I want not a single Negro for other purpose than his immediate liberation. I consider every individual thus unshackled as the source of future generations, not to say nations, of freemen; and I shudder when I think that so insignificant an animal as I am is invested with this monstrous, this horrid power."

So many were the manumissions of which these are typical, that, by 1790, there were more than 35,000 freedmen in the South. And while the reasons assigned were changed in the Nineteenth Century, liberations on a large scale were made. A unique sample was that of John McDonogh, the most thrifty citizen of New Orleans in his day, who made a bargain with his whole force of slaves, about 1825, by which they were collectively to earn their freedom and their passage to Liberia by their overtime work on Saturday afternoons. This labor was to be done in McDonogh's own service, and he was to keep account of their earnings. They were entitled to draw upon this fund upon approved occasions; but, since the contract was with the whole group of slaves as a unit, when one applied for cash, the others must draw theirs *pro rata*, thereby postponing the common day of liberation. Any slaves violating the rules of good conduct were to be sold by the master, whereupon their accrued earnings would revert to the fund of the rest. The plan was carried to completion on schedule; and, after some delay in embarkation, they left America in 1842, some eighty in number, with their late master's benediction. In concluding his public narration, McDonogh wrote: "They have now sailed for Liberia, the land of their fathers. I can say with truth and heartfelt satisfaction that a more virtuous people does not exist in any country."

There were also not a few families of Virginia and South Carolina who, though not without difficulties, colonized their Negroes in Ohio, and themselves, in some cases, began life afresh as pioneers in a new country.

Sometimes the liberations were attended with romance, as, when Pierre Chastang, of Mobile, was bought and freed by popular subscription in recognition of public services in the War of 1812 and in the yellow fever epidemic of 1819. Another outstanding figure was Sam whose freedom was bought in reward for his saving the State Capitol from burning, the Georgia Legislature providing $1800 by a special act for this purpose. Negroes freed for meritorious service, and those buying their own freedom, became ensamples of substantial worth to the free population.

Among these freedmen there were some notable figures who, for one cause or another, were highly esteemed in the locality in which they lived. Just two examples must suffice. "In Georgia, the most notable was Austin Dabney, who, as a mulatto youth, served in the Revolutionary Army and attached himself ever after to the white family who saved his life when he was wounded in battle. The Georgia legislature, by special act, gave him a farm; he was welcomed in the tavern circle of chatting lawyers whenever his favorite, Judge Dooly, held court in his home village; and once, when the formality of drawing his pension carried him to Savannah, the Governor of the State, seeing him pass, invited him as a guest in his house.

In 1792, a Negro named Caesar, noted for his knowledge of curative herbs, was liberated by purchase, the Assembly of South Carolina voting the funds and, in addition, an annuity for life.

Thus, by purchase, manumission and natural growth, the 35,000 Free Negroes of 1790 grew to approximately a half million in 1860—about equally divided between the North and the South. The chief concentration was in the Border States, the number rapidly decreasing with increasing distance from the middle line. The climate and the industrial repression in the far North were alike unwholesome to this class; and the suspicion and stringent laws in the far South about as much so. In both cases the Whites had the upper hand, and in both cases they used their power after their own wills.

The lot of the freedmen was, indeed, a difficult one to bear. The philosophy of the Negro, and the habit of association, were certainly chief elements in the preservation of peace to a remarkable degree. The well-to-do had their property at stake; the large majority of day laborers, the unprosperous and inert, were satisfied simply to be free. It was the smaller class, within the class, who represented the progressive freedmen, the forerunners and prophets of the after-war leaders and seers of the race. For these forerunners had already, in their day, entered every large field of endeavor which engages the race of today.

Among the Churches, in the North, with few exceptions, the freedman was driven to form his own organizations; while, in the South, he was encouraged to adopt the churches of the Whites; indeed, in the South, few separate churches were provided by any denominations.

Among the fraternal organizations, he had none in the South in common with the Whites; while, in the North, the Masons and Odd Fellows were introduced, the latter through a Negro initiate who had been received in England. This most natural and important feature of Negro social life was, for the most part, supplied by their own secret societies. These were very numerous all over the land, as they are at this day. It is quite impossible to get accurately at the history of these societies, so screened in secrecy. A mere glimpse may be had of their purpose through the published notes on the

"Union Band Society of New Orleans," 1860. Its motto was "Love, Union, Peace," its officers were of both sexes. Members were pledged to obey the laws of the Lodge, and its officers were pledged to keep its secrets, to live in love and union with its members, to visit one another and the sick, to report illnesses of members, and to wear the regalia when required. The Official Mother was required to assign nurses for the sick who were looked after in every detail. Funeral expenses and the burial, in minute detail, were provided for. (We may note, parenthetically, that, while secret societies are the rule in every African tribe, it is doubtful if these had more than a remote connection with the societies in America.)

In the public schools, the Negro freedmen were little regarded. In the North, generally, they were debarred from the white schools, and poorly provided with schools of their own; in the South, after 1840, education was discouraged, and, in most communities, forbidden.

The Fugitive-Slave Law bred great irregularity and injustice to the freedmen. The occasion was thus made for kidnapping the free Negroes, transporting them to distant regions where identification would be difficult, and the subsequent sale of the captives or their involuntary servitude. Societies were established, here and there, to prevent these heartrending tragedies. All the States had laws against it, and practically no failure to convict is recorded when the offender was brought to judgment. But the crime was so comparatively easy, that the wonder is, that the freedmen increased so steadily and normally.

An interesting phase of the life of the freedman is illustrated by the census of urban workers. The United States Census of 1850 gives, in parallel columns, the occupations of free colored labor, above 15 years of age, in New York and New Orleans, respectively. In the former there were 3,337, and in the latter 1,792. New York had 4 lawyers and 3 druggists, New Orleans none; the ministers were 21 to 1; the physicians, 9 to 4; merchants, 3 to 64; jewelers, 3 to 5; clerks, 7 to 61; teachers, 8 to 12. New Orleans also had 4 capitalists, 2 planters, 11 overseers, 9 grocers, and 2 collectors, while New York had none of these. New York had three times as many barbers as New Orleans, and twice as many butchers; but, while New Orleans had 355 carpenters, New York had only 12, and no masons as against 278 for New Orleans. A like proportion was shown in all the skilled trades.

In New York, one-third of the freedmen were unskilled laborers; while, in New Orleans, barely a tenth were of this class. This was due to the greater discrimination against colored labor in the North, which was true then as now. The laws in various Northern States excluded free immigrants, and discriminated against those who were already in their borders. In industrial life, they were very generally excluded from the trades. On the other hand, in the South, while the laws were even more severe, they were interpreted far more leniently, and the practice of the Whites was more kindly, with the result revealed in the Census quoted.

In view of the difficult condition of the freedman, it is remarkable that so few accepted the invitations, so widely given, to emigrate to other and free lands. The Colonization Society offered facilities to move to Liberia, beginning with 1819; the Haitien Government offered special inducement in 1824 and again in 1859, even promising free transportation and free lands to the French-speaking Negroes of Louisiana. In 1840, an Immigration Society offered free transportation to British Guiana. But few availed themselves of these opportunities, preferring the ills they suffered, along with very general security and prosperity to those they knew not of in the distant lands.

It is also remarkable that so few real uprisings against the white slave-holders should have occurred. These were generally led by the freedmen, and many are reported; but, in most cases, the reports were much like the flaring headlines of a modern newspaper, and must be attributed to the nervous dread of such possibilities. This, more than the few real happenings, led to the enactment of stringent laws; but the generally harmonious life was rewarded with very lax execution of such laws. In truth, the proportion of slave-holding, free Negroes in some localities, such as New Orleans and Charleston, too nearly approached that of the white slave-holders, to warrant a persistent suspicion of danger. In spite of all these difficulties, a few free Negroes of note, both men and women, appear in every generation.

Dr. James Derham, born a slave in Philadelphia in 1762, became the slave of a physician in New Orleans, who trained and used him as an assistant. He bought his freedom, and became the first recognized Negro physician of whom there is record. "Dr. Benjamin Rush," says the *Negro Year Book*, "the celebrated physician, published an account of Derham and spoke in the highest terms of his character and skill as a physician."

Dr. Kelly Miller tells us that "the first real impetus to bring free Negroes in considerable numbers into the professional world, came from the American Colonization Society which, in the early years, flourished in the South, as well as in the North ... and undertook to prepare professional leaders of their race for the Liberian Colony." The Society began its work about 1817, and sent teachers, trained in the South and the North alike, to the Colony established shortly after. Among these teachers were Doctors Taylor, Fleet, and DeGrasse.

A century earlier, Benjamin Banneker, born in Baltimore in 1731, was the first man in America to make a clock which struck the hours.

Phyllis Wheatley, born in Africa, and brought to Boston where she was sold to John Wheatley, and educated, wrote verses which were highly endorsed. They were published in London, and covered a variety of topics, religious and moral chiefly. To these names of Negroes who attained distinction, should be added that of Daniel A. Payne, of Baltimore, the founder of Union Seminary (consolidated in 1863 with Wilberforce University), who became a Bishop of the African Methodist Church. Others will appear in our study of the religious development of the race.

Commercially, the freedmen were not without conspicuous examples of thrift and material success. There was "John Jones, the colored proprietor of a popular hotel in Charleston, who lived in the same manner as his white patrons, accumulated property to the value of some $40,000, and maintained a reputation for high business integrity and talent." Others there were among the free people of that city, respected and prosperous, with considerable establishments served by slaves. In New Orleans, a still larger number of wealthy colored people lived. Thomy Lafon, a merchant and money lender, was distinguished both for his wealth and philanthropy. He died about 30 years ago at the age of 82, leaving an estate valued at nearly half a million, from which many charities benefited. Unfortunately, wealth and good repute are not indissolubly united anywhere or among any people; it is therefore pleasant to recall them wedded in the person of a Negro.

Many of the freedmen were gifted in small trades, and even when laws were passed excluding them from populous slave-areas, petitions were common requesting that worthy ones might be permitted to remain. On the seaboard, boating and fishing provided, on a small scale, both a profitable and a free life for many. A few cases of large slave and land-holding appear, particularly in Louisiana. Cyprian Ricard bought at Sheriff's Sale, in 1851, an estate in Iberville Parish, at a cost of nearly a quarter of a million dollars. "Marie Metoyer, of Nachitoches Parish, had fifty-eight slaves, and more than two thousand acres of land when she died in 1840." There were others in Louisiana, as well as in South Carolina, Virginia and Maryland.

These conditions among the freedmen as well as the patriarchal system on the plantations had their results in the development of the race.

Along with, and under the tuition of, the pioneers of America, the Negro cleared the forests, drained the swamps, subdued the wild lands, built the homes and absorbed the civilization of the older race which he served. Here, as always, service of others was the highest service of self; for, conscious or otherwise, all service has its reaction upon the servers. What the older races got, through the long, weary, successive preparations of the ages of stone and wood and iron; of slave and feudal and chivalric and democratic eras; that, in contact with the highest form of which America was capable, the ablest and most diligent among the Negroes got through their amazing capacity for absorption and adaptability. To those who know the Negro best, this capacity for adaptation and absorption is still unbelievable; while to those who know him remotely, it is a miracle, unexplained or misconstrued. To the former—his white friends of the South through three centuries of intimate association—the difficulty is to understand what their eyes behold—a child-race of seventy years ago already producing leaders who stand among their people as clear, true ensigns of their race. To the latter—the man who knows the Negro more

REMOTELY—THE MIRACLE IS EXPLAINED ONLY UPON THE ASSUMPTION THAT THE NEGRO IS A CAUCASIAN IN BLACK AND NOT WHAT GOD MADE HIM—A NEGRO—WITH HIS OWN RACIAL CHARACTERISTICS, ABLE TO ABSORB WHAT IS BEST IN THE WORLD, TO BUILD IT UNTO HIMSELF AND TO STAND BEFORE HIS MASTER AND BEFORE MANKIND IN GOD AND SELF-FASHIONED BLACK MANHOOD.

THE SCIENTIFIC PROFESSIONS HAVE BEEN ENTERED BY EVER-INCREASING NUMBERS AND BY INCREASINGLY BETTER-TRAINED MEN; BY WOMEN, TOO, THOUGH IN SMALLER NUMBERS. DOCTORS, LAWYERS, INVENTORS, CHEMISTS, SCHOLARS, EDITORS, SOME WORTHY TO RANK HIGH IN THEIR PROFESSIONS, AND SOME KNOWN ON BOTH SIDES OF THE OCEAN, ARE AT ONCE THE PRIDE OF THEIR RACE, AND THE MINISTERS TO ITS MANY NEEDS.

THERE WERE TRIBES IN AFRICA, WHICH PRODUCED MEN OF DECIDED ARTISTIC TALENT, UNTRAINED. THEY ARE REPRESENTED HERE IN THE COTERIE OF WORTHY SCULPTORS AND PAINTERS. ALL WERE MUSICIANS, RUDE DOUBTLESS IN THEIR NATIVE HAUNTS, BUT ALWAYS PLAINTIVE. THESE, TOO, ARE HERE, EVERYWHERE SOFTENED AND SWEETENED IN A GENTLER ATMOSPHERE, AND IN HIGHEST CULTURE PRODUCING A BLACK PATTI, A FISH QUARTETTE, AND OTHERS OF LIKE GIFTS. IT MAY NOT BE TO THE CREDIT OF COMPOSER OR PLAYER, BUT THE FASHIONABLE (AND ABOMINABLE) RAG-TIME MUSIC IS THEIR GIFT TO THE WORLD. IN POETRY, PAUL LAWRENCE DUNBAR IS UNIVERSALLY READ AND SUNG, AND THERE ARE MANY OTHERS ALMOST AS WORTHY. IN FICTION, A MORNING PAPER OF DECEMBER 14, 1921, ANNOUNCES THE WINNER OF THE PRIZE OF THE GINCOURT ACADEMY, PARIS, AS RENÉ MORAN, A NEGRO NOVELIST OF THE ISLAND OF MARTINIQUE. AMERICA, IN SPITE OF BLOTS, HERE AND THERE, HAS BEEN KIND TO THE NEGRO, HAS GIVEN HIM A CHANCE, HAS HELPED HIM TO EMBRACE IT, HAS TAUGHT HIM MUCH, AND LEARNED SOMEWHAT FROM HIM.

Chapter V
THE PERIOD OF WAR AND RECONSTRUCTION

We have seen the results of the patriarchal system under which the Negro lived in America during the slave era. Then, with the four long years of war, followed by the eleven (in one State fifteen) long, weary years of Reconstruction, came the day of testing of the results of the carefully built up family and trade-school training.

Regarding the war-period and the result of its testing, white and Negro alike agree. No one is better qualified to speak of it than the one Negro who knew, and who, more than any man of his day, is entitled to the credit and the honor of fashioning out of the past a new and greatly better era for his people and his country, Dr. Booker T. Washington.

He writes: "The self-control which the Negro exhibited during the war marks, it seems to me, one of the most important chapters in the history of the race. Notwithstanding that he knew his master was away from home fighting a battle which, if successful, would result in his continued enslavement, yet he worked faithfully for the support of his master's family. If the Negro had yielded to the temptation and suggestion to use the torch or dagger in an attempt to destroy his master's property or family, the result would have been that the war would have been quickly ended; for the master would have returned from the battlefield to protect and defend his property and family. But the Negro, to the last, was faithful to the trust that had been thrust upon him, and during the four years of war, there is not a single instance recorded where he attempted in any way to outrage the family or to injure his master's property."

His white friends have said as much. Thomas Nelson Page writes: "It is to the eternal credit of the Whites and of the Negroes that, during the four years of war, when the white men of the South were absent in the field, they could entrust their wives, their children, all they possessed, to the care and guardianship of their slaves with absolute confidence in their fidelity." And again: "They raised the crop that fed the

Confederate Army, and suffered without complaint the privations which came alike to White and Black."

Those who experienced it all solemnly and sacredly acknowledge the debt of gratitude to that generation of Negro servants which they as sacredly bequeathed to their posterity. Said a father to his son, thirty-four years after emancipation, as death was closing his eyes, "Son, see that my old Black people are cared for." This was his sole dying injunction.

But what is the significance of the testing of war? It meant that Africans who, in their native land, had acknowledged no obligation to anybody outside of tribal ties, whose habit of life had been constant warfare with all else, had been transformed by new family ties which embraced, in loyal fidelity, White and Black alike. It meant that savage people, who had owned no sense of responsibility save that which protected personal life and furthered personal wishes, had been so wonderfully tutored as to expand that sense of responsibility into a loyalty of trust that is little short of miraculous. A war whose issue was the Negro's freedom, could not break that bond of trust. So far, in the character of its product—both White and Negro—the old family and trade-school had been tested, and the examination had been passed. When the war closed, the old friendship was as strong as ever, and the mutual relation closer than ever. In most cases, their freedom was first announced to their former slaves by the old masters; and both together set about the establishment of the new relations with hearty good will and the united desire "to re-build our homes."

Then came the Reconstruction Period, with its testing of a very different nature. Here again, let us hear what the Negro has to say, and learn from himself his response. Dr. Washington writes: "At the close of the war, both the Southern white man and the Negro found themselves in the midst of poverty. The ex-master returned from the war to find his slave-property gone, his farms and other industries in a state of collapse, and the whole industrial and economic system, upon which he had depended for years, entirely disorganized.

As we review, calmly and dispassionately, the period of Reconstruction, we must use a great deal of sympathy and generosity. The weak point, to my mind, in the Reconstruction era was that no strong force was brought to bear in the direction of preparing the Negro to become an intelligent, reliable citizen and voter. The main effort seemed to have been in the direction of controlling his vote for the time being, regardless of future interests. I hardly believe that any race of people, with similar preparation and similar surroundings, would have acted more wisely than, or very differently from, the way the Negro acted during the period of Reconstruction.... I do not believe that the Negro was so much at fault for entering so largely into politics, and for the mistakes that were made in too many cases, as were the unscrupulous white leaders who got the Negro's confidence, and controlled his vote, to further their own ends, regardless, in many cases, of the permanent welfare of the Negro. I have always considered it unfortunate that the Southern white man did not make more effort during the period of Reconstruction to get the confidence and sympathy of the Negro, and thus have been able to keep him in close touch and sympathy in politics.... What the Negro wants, and what the country wants to do, is to take advantage of all the lessons that were taught during the days of Reconstruction, and apply these lessons bravely and honestly in laying the foundation upon which the Negro can stand in the future, and make himself a useful, honorable and desirable citizen, whether he has his new residence in the North, the South, or the West."

The description is true. The white friend would have written this one sentence differently—"I have always considered it unfortunate that the Southern white man did not make more effort—to get the confidence of the Negro...." The misfortune was, that the old Southern friends were not permitted to retain the confidence of their old Negro friends who were estranged and filled with suspicion by the same "unscrupulous white leaders who got the Negro's confidence—to further their own ends." Time and time again, during this era, far-seeing Southerners, sometimes against the vigorous protest of their neighbors, offered small farms to their old servants at very low prices, which would provide homes of self-respect and stem the tide of temptation to wander and to idle about. Not a few accepted the advice of their old and best friends; but the new toy of ownership was too alluring. In nearly all cases the feeling of wealth in possession bred spendthrift habits and the early loss of the farms.

But our purpose is not to trace the story of Reconstruction. This has been amply told by Southerners—Thomas Nelson Page and others; and by Northerners—Carl Schurz, Rhodes and others. Our purpose is to note the result of this testing-time upon the pupils trained in the old plantation trade-school.

Again the answer is given by Dr. Washington, whose testimony is substantially that of his race of that generation. "This business contact with the Southern white man, and the industrial training received on the plantations, put the Negro, at the close of the war, into possession of all the common and skilled labor of the South. For nearly twenty years after the war, except in one or two cases, the value of the industrial training given by the Negroes' former masters on the plantations and elsewhere was overlooked. Negro men and women were educated in literature, mathematics and the sciences, with no thought of what had taken place on these plantations for two and one half centuries. After twenty years, those who were trained as mechanics, etc., during slavery, began to disappear by death; and gradually we awoke to the fact that we had no one to take their places. We had scores of young men learned in Greek; but few in carpentry, or mechanical or architectural drawing. We had trained many in Latin; but almost none as engineers, bridge-builders, and machinists. Numbers were taken from the farm and educated, but were educated in everything else except agriculture. Hence they had no sympathy with farm life, and did not return to it."

The real fact is, that, as a result of the Reconstruction policies, quite fifteen years were well nigh lost in the development of the Negro. For what is the value of tuition in Greek and Latin and the finer arts, for a few of the brighter minds—so few as barely to touch the fringe of the great race—compared with the prevailing temporary loss of the advantages of generations of training in practical arts, the racial estrangement in their old homes, and the long years of protected idleness and sloth such as Carl Schurz describes?

During this Reconstruction Period, the religious life as well as the industrial life of the Negro was disturbed and oftentimes destroyed with a resultant loss in the development of good citizenship.

The condition of the Church in the South, where so vast a majority of the Negroes were destined to retain their homes, is beyond a healthy imagination now to picture. The armies of the long years of war had swept over them from Virginia to Texas. The Rev. Bowyer Stewart, in his *Hale Memorial Sermon* of 1913, gives a summary, the accuracy of which may be accepted. In Virginia, some 14 churches were destroyed, and 24 more or less damaged; in South Carolina, 13 churches destroyed, and 26 chapels for Negroes; in Tennessee, only 3 churches escaped injury; while in Georgia, Alabama, Mississippi, Arkansas and Louisiana, the conditions were somewhat worse than in North Carolina. The many churches and schools put to military use, meant the destruction of furniture and the abuse of buildings, which rendered the latter useless for the time. Episcopal residences and rectories, in some cases, suffered either total or partial destruction. The poverty was very great. A careful examination, reported to the South Carolina Convention, in 1868, showed that "along the entire seaboard, from North Carolina to Georgia, where our Church had flourished for more than a century, there are but four parishes which maintain religious services; not one, outside the city of Charleston, can be called a living, self-sustaining parish; their clergy live by fishing, farming and mechanic arts." Other Dioceses, though in less measure, as a rule, experienced great loss and great poverty.

But there were great men at the helm—Bishops Johns, Atkinson, Davis (soon succeeded by Howe), Elliott, the two Wilmers, Quintard, Lay, and Gregg. The five years to 1871, showed recovery of white communicants in nearly every Diocese except South Carolina. All alike had lost many of their Negro members, the greatest loss being in South Carolina which originally had most. South Carolina, however, is a fairly typical illustration of the comparative loss of Negro members throughout the South. In 1861, the Diocesan Journal records 2979 white communicants and 2973 colored; that of 1872, 3102 white, 618 colored, most of these in Calvary Church and St. Mark's, Charleston.

Why was this? The facts are the more astonishing when one reflects upon the universal practice of the Church, during so many generations, of close religious association; upon the success of Christian teaching so apparently universal upon the complete trust in one another exhibited during the test of war; and the resultant feeling of affectionate gratitude on the part of the white Churchmen.

Moreover, the latter were prepared to continue the Christian ministrations under the new order in the confident expectation that, however changed the economic and social relation, nothing could sever the bond of Christian fellowship in the Church. Bishop Davis, in 1866, was expressing a conviction universally shared when, looking out upon the vast confusion, he nevertheless declared, "I have not complete statistics; but am convinced, from observation and information, that, in all cases where the colored population shall be reinstated in their former localities, they will return to the communion of the Church." Unfortunately, however, succeeding years bore testimony to progressive losses, until another Bishop voiced the thought which experience, in turn, had universally brought: "The defection from the Church is almost universal. In some parishes I have visited, which a few years ago numbered more than a hundred communicants, not one has come forward to kneel at the altar, and very few to enter the church. The voice of remonstrance from their once-honored pastors falls unheeded upon their ears; unscriptural revelation are substituted for the Word of God; the ancient forms of worship are declared to quench the ministrations of the Spirit; and the sober worship of the sanctuary is exchanged for the midnight orgies of a frantic superstition." There are some very bright and cheering exceptions, but this quotation from Bishop Wilmer, of Louisiana, describes the rule.

Why was it? The question may not be answered in a short phrase, and probably may not be answered satisfactorily at all.

There was the fact that the Negro's religious teachers had been his masters, beloved under the old régime, but whose guidance and control, even in church, was to be regarded with wary suspicion. He could not differentiate between the essential wrong of a system, and the blessing which the

Church had brought to him in that system. For the present, the wrong was uppermost in his mind.

Then there was the Reconstruction system, and the hope held, in confident expectation, of a change in condition which a changed social relation would miraculously effect. The Negro masses could not foresee the slow, toilsome pathway up which every primitive race has plodded to changed conditions, and better.

Again, there was the natural conviction of the Negro that his freed allegiance was now due to his Northern liberators; and this, beyond any bond of slave-time friendship with those who had held him in slavery. It was the newborn freedom, from restraint, entering like new wine into old vessels overstrained.

Finally, there was among the few Negro leaders, (and, because few, therefore all the more powerful) the exultant and alluring ambition to play the man, and to attempt to demonstrate the full-grown majority of a race just dropping its swaddling clothes.

These were the conditions (inevitable to the change of social structure from slave to free) ready at hand when the Reconstruction policies offered the chance to unscrupulous politicians from North and South. They offered a ready opportunity for inspiring the Negro with a subtle distrust of former masters now become neighbors. Racial hatred for the wrongs of slavery, now became magnified to the exclusion of any benefits whatever derived from the system. For the unscrupulous, the rewards increased with the widening of the chasm between race and race; they were secured at the price of the ruthless exploitation of the Negroes, and the breeding of a spirit of suspicion and distrust toward their old friends.

To the positive and infallible declarations to the Negroes that allegiance to the Church of their masters meant the continuation of slavery, the great racial instinct, as yet untutored to know better, responded with tremendous and deep fervor. Only the few could know better, and have the courage to follow their own convictions. And what else could have been possible in view of the actual conditions? Had wiser counsels prevailed, and had old racial and personal attachments and interdependencies, so carefully

BUILT UP, BEEN FOSTERED AS THE BEST CONDITION UNDER WHICH TO WORK OUT THE STUPENDOUS PROBLEMS OF THE NEW TIME, NO ONE CAN DOUBT THAT THE STORY OF AMERICAN LIFE WOULD HAVE BEEN DIFFERENT, AND FEW CAN DOUBT THAT IT WOULD HAVE BEEN BETTER. AS IT WAS, THE CONDITIONS WHICH SERVED THE UNWORTHY ENDS OF THE WHITE DEMAGOGUE, WERE SADLY FRUITFUL IN HEARTRENDING RESULTS UPON THE RELIGION OF THE NEGRO.

FOR MANY, THERE WAS THE CLINGING MEMORY OF HEATHEN SUPERSTITIONS—HARDLY ASLEEP—CERTAINLY NOT DEAD. THERE WAS THE "CALL OF THE WILD"—POWERFUL OVER ALL NATURE, HOWEVER HIGHLY DEVELOPED—AND NOW HEARD BY A PEOPLE ONLY JUST FREED FROM THE LEASH. WHAT RACE IN ALL HISTORY HAS EVER FACED SUCH SUDDEN, SUCH POWERFUL TEMPTATIONS AS WERE FREELY CAST BEFORE THIS PEOPLE, BACKED UP BY MILITARY OCCUPANCY? THE AMAZING THING IS, THAT THEY STOOD BEFORE SUCH TEMPTATIONS WITH AS LITTLE RESULTING HARM TO THEMSELVES AND TO THE WHITES AS MAY JUSTLY BE CHARGED AGAINST EITHER.

IT WAS NOT ALONE, OR EVEN CHIEFLY, THAT THIS WAS MADE POSSIBLE BY PRECAUTIONS TO PREVENT RACIAL CLASHES. IT WAS, BEFORE EVERYTHING ELSE, BECAUSE OF THE TWO CENTURIES OF AMERICAN LIFE IN WHICH THE NEGROES HAD MORE AND MORE PROGRESSED IN ALL THAT GOES TO TRANSFORM HEATHEN SAVAGES INTO CHRISTIAN MEN AND WOMEN, AND HAD EARNED THE RIGHT OF TRUST AND AFFECTION WITHOUT THE CLOGGING BURDEN OF VAST RESPONSIBILITY IMPOSSIBLE OF FULFILMENT. DR. WASHINGTON IS RIGHT WHEN HE SAYS, AS ALREADY NOTED, "I DO NOT BELIEVE THAT THE NEGRO WAS SO MUCH AT FAULT ... FOR THE MISTAKES THAT WERE MADE IN TOO MANY CASES, AS WERE THE UNSCRUPULOUS WHITE LEADERS WHO GOT THE NEGROES' CONFIDENCE ... TO FURTHER THEIR OWN ENDS."

THOSE YEARS OF ASSOCIATION HAD PRODUCED THEIR INTIMATE, CONFIDENTIAL FRIENDSHIPS BETWEEN THE WHITE MASTER AND THE STRONG HEAD-MEN ON EVERY PLANTATION—FRIENDSHIPS WHICH NOTHING COULD DESTROY; AND EVERY COMMUNITY POINTS BACK TO LEVEL HEADED, WISE, OLDER NEGROES WHO SAW, THOUGH THEY COULD NOT FULLY MEASURE, THE SERIOUSNESS BROUGHT BY THE NEW DAY. THE QUIET, ALMOST SECRET CONFERENCES OF THESE OLD FRIENDS ABOUT THE NEW LIFE, ENTERED AS LEAVEN INTO THE GREAT UNLEAVENED, WORKING, DISMAYED MASS. THE BREAK BECAME A CHASM AS RECONSTRUCTION ADVANCED. THE RACE HAD NOT YET HAD TIME TO BECOME ESTABLISHED.

We must note, too, that slavery, however serviceable in the discipline of a new people, did not conduce to self-reliance in any walk of life; it was not the favorable condition out of which to develop steadfastness in the religious life so essential to desirable citizenship. "The law is the schoolmaster to lead to Christ," is not only the terse description of a long episode in the history of our religious forefathers, it is still more the expression of the law of religious growth. First, there is the period of the imposition of law, with its tuition of restraint from without, gradually developing into self-imposed control as the sense of the reasonable justice and righteousness of it develops. Then the habit of balanced self-restraint, as the motive of righteousness, becomes instinct with life through the growth of the Christ-life in us, when the pattern life is the only life dominant over conscience.

To have expected this process to be completed, and its fruits full-grown, in any considerable number of this newly, partially converted people, was certainly unreasonable. It is our complaint of our own race, that, after more than twelve centuries of inherited Christian faith, we are so far from this consummation. At the very best, slavery was the reign of law, but with no settled objective toward the full "liberty of the children of God"; and as long as St. Paul's law of development was arrested in mid-operation, it had scant chance of complete fruition.

In an age of progressive education through the printed page, this accepted means of hastening tuition in religious knowledge and spiritual character, was withheld from the slave as inapplicable, even dangerous, to his condition. While it may be recalled that Christianity flourished before printing, it is enough to say that human progress is the product of its own age, and the condition of an age retards him who declines or is deprived of conformity to it, as readily as it stimulates him who conforms.

Such is our attempt to explain the very great defection of the Negro from the white Churches after the war. Doubtless it falls short of being a complete explanation, but it seems to be at least a natural one.

The year 1880 may properly be considered as marking the close of the period of the War and Reconstruction. With exceptions noted later, the period was one of consternation to the leaders of the Church, and deep regret over what seemed the failure of the long years of devoted ministry; for the Negro race had shown retrogression in every way, religiously, morally, and industrially. Those twenty years of lost opportunity of which Dr. Washington wrote, were lost to all save the very few who were strong enough to yield themselves to the best influences, and steadfastly to build that best into themselves. To the Church leaders of the day, all seemed lost. But was all lost? The answer of faith is an emphatic NO!

The Episcopal Church lost uncounted numbers of members. Some of these doubtless were never shepherded to any earthly fold. Most of them, with no education to add power to a half-formed faith, became partial victims of the temptations of traditional heathen religions. But the newly born and developing faith was not lost, even though the Fathers' anxiety and profound distress over the lapse of spiritual children to "indications of African barbarism" are pathetic excuse for their despair. It would have been as unnatural for the Whites to measure the full significance of this day of complete revolution in the life of the Negroes, as for the Negroes to escape the first consequences of it. Nor was it possible for such an era to end in a day. Other peoples have had revolutions, and with like results. The French Revolution, with nearly 1700 years of Christian training behind its victims, and its consequences still a factor of no small power in French life, is a pointed instance. Indeed eras, good or bad, do not really end; they carry forward and onward. The era of Reconstruction carried onward in American life; and, in like manner, the era of Slavery, with its mingled beneficence and cruelty, its Christian and industrial training intertwined with heathen traditions, its régime of earnest, zealous, loving ministry, its "line upon line and precept upon precept" of unwearying tuition—this, too, for better or worse, influenced the Negro of a later period. When, at length, the excesses inevitably connected with the new-found freedom had ceased, and when the years of loss had come to an end, then the old training, religious and industrial, and the need for its power in racial development came once more to the fore in the minds of these few truly great and conspicuous leaders whose lives spanned the great gulf of past and present. These were able to wrest much of

ADVANTAGE TO THEIR RACE OUT OF THE VERY MISTAKES IN EDUCATION WHICH DR. WASHINGTON LAMENTS.

We have reminded ourselves of the tremendous, the indescribably difficult, task of the very small band of Negro leaders, in guiding their people to a saner life and to the ambition to fill life with the best that God's gifts to them would enable. Of such, were Bishop Payne, of the African Methodist Church; John Jasper, the famous Richmond preacher; Alexander Crummell, of the Episcopal Church; Henry M. Turner, of the African Methodist Church; Isaiah Montgomery, of Mount Bayou, Mississippi; and, of the younger men, Booker T. Washington and his successor Robert R. Moton, Archdeacon Russell, Dr. Bragg, Dr. Tunnell, Dr. DuBois, Bishop Demby, Professor Battle, and many others of their generation. What a load they have had to carry as represented by ignorance, superstition, low moral tone, shiftlessness and unresponse in the vast majority of their brethren! What a task, to overcome the losses of that very era which produced their younger men! What a supreme faith, what unswerving confidence in their great mission, were demanded, and in large measure provided! We can but reflect that, whether or no the Whites recognize the wisdom of the methods and philosophies of one or all or any of the Negro leaders, the greatest sin we can commit toward them is to withhold our sympathy from them in their toilsome, troublous, tragic, upward pathway along which, with sweat of blood, they must lead the millions of their brethren. The demand of their condition, ever since Reconstruction, has been, and is now, for that patient, helpful sympathy from which confidence is born, the confidence which invites mutual conference, the correction of error, the enlightenment of motive and objective, and so on to a common task to which White and Negro alike can devote their best efforts.

As Dr. Washington says, it was too late to cry over what might have been. The era produced at least one institution (possibly there may have been others) which a wise head conceived—Hampton Institute, Virginia. General Armstrong, with equally wise retrospect and foresight, built upon the past for an enduring future—a future that would restore the best in the past, and make the best better. Hampton would have been a success even had it died after producing Booker

T. Washington, founder of Tuskegee Institute; and James S. Russell, founder of St Paul's School, Lawrenceville, Va.

There was something, too, that the Reconstruction Era could not destroy. It could fan racial prejudices, and set race against race in political antagonism; but it could not destroy the deep, ever abiding affections between the races, which the old life had nurtured. That remained as both the motive for redeeming the time, and the foundation for the rebuilded life so sadly shattered and dismembered. The era ended, white and black again took up the task of rebuilding.

Of the total negro population, in 1880, about 95 per cent were still in the South; and, in 1920, after forty years of development, and in spite of the enticement of the fabulous wages in manufacturing States created by the World War, this percentage is still nearly 75 per cent. The South is the Negro's home, and the conditions of his greatest opportunity are there. This is the testimony of both black and white observers. Read Edgar Gardner Murphy's *Problems of the Present South* (p. 184 *et seq.*); DuBois's *The Philadelphia Negro*; and this passage from the address by the Principal of Tuskegee which, in short, expresses the witness of all alike: "Wherever the Negro has lost ground, industrially, in the South, it is not because there is prejudice against him, as a skilled laborer, on the part of the native Southern white man.... There is almost no prejudice, against the Negro in the South in matters of business, so far as the native Whites are concerned." This was published in 1899. Since then, Labor Unions have had a disconcerting relation to the matter—a relation still in solution. But certainly there was a free field for the Negro for about half a century, coupled with about as much help from the white people as they could give and as the Negro would seek; from the Northern White also, about as much as the Negro could profitably use. The results of these fifty years seem to prove this, and to offer irrefutable evidence of the excellent preparatory work of the old patriarchal system which we have reviewed in a previous chapter.

Chapter VI
THE EDUCATION OF THE NEGRO

We have studied the Negro, both slave and free, in his native home and when transplanted. We have looked upon the picture which his life exhibits under these varying conditions. We have traced his career through the school of slavery into the larger school of free American life, and seen the picture which his life has wrought here. We turn now to the forces which have produced a transformation not short of startling to the casual observer. The two forces are education, which occupies this chapter, and the Christian religion which will engage us in the next.

Among the educated colonists of the early years, there was no question raised as to the education of slaves. Schools were few for themselves, and in most cases instruction in letters fell among family duties. Slaves were as yet indentured servants, few in number, and were probably taught, if at all, along with the children of the family. Intelligent masters naturally regarded intelligent servants as most profitable to their mutual interest. Unlettered owners quite as naturally had neither the wish nor the ability to instruct their servants in letters, and both alike enjoyed the freedom from such mental strain.

As the population—free and slave—increased, and as social life became more complex and the status of the slaves fixed, questions as to the education of the latter were raised. The cultured slave-holders very generally, and the missionaries universally, contended for their education; the exploiters and materialists usually opposed it; though there may have been exceptions on both sides. It was not until after the insurrectionary movements around 1835, that laws against Negro education were possible because upheld by public sentiment. By this time it was very generally feared that ability to read would be the ready means of learning of uprisings abroad and of suggesting them at home.

Perhaps the earliest systematic effort toward Negro education was in 1691, when, in Virginia, the Church became the agency through which the apprenticeship of Negroes was made. Youths gifted mechanically and industrially were indentured on condition that the talent be developed and that they be taught to read; in some cases "to read the Bible distinctly" was specified. Both before and after that date, there is abundant evidence that parochial instruction was not unusual by the missionaries, especially in the Southern Colonies.

In 1704, Elias Neau, a French Protestant, who had come to New York and conformed to the English Church, opened a school for the Negroes. Success attended his efforts; but, in 1712, attempts were made to close his school as contributing to insurrectionary movements. Mr. Neau was able to prove that only one of his pupils had joined such a movement, and the school continued its good work under successive teachers and rectors for more than half a century. Originally this school was under the auspices of the Society for the Propagation of the Gospel ("S. P. G."), but later it came under parochial support, presumably that of Trinity Church.

The S. P. G. required of its teachers that the Negroes and Indians be taught to read the Bible and other useful books and poems, and be grounded in the Church Catechism. Some three years before the opening of the Neau School, the Rev. Samuel Thomas had established an S. P. G. school in Goose Creek Parish, S. C. Mr. Thomas in his account of the one thousand slaves in his parish, reported that many of them could read the Bible distinctly. Gradually schools were here and there dotted over the colonies, in connection with the churches.

The most ambitious enterprise of these early years, was the school established in Charleston, about 1741. Two slaves were bought, Harry and Andrew, selected for their unusual intelligence, and trained to be the teachers of others, and especially of slaves who could carry back to their homes the learning acquired. Commissary Garden erected the building and launched the school with about sixty young students at the opening. The promoters planned to send out annually from thirty to forty youths as teachers. Unhappily its life was short, less than twenty-five years.

About the same time the Catechetical Schools in St. Peter's and Christ Church, Philadelphia, were opened with William

Sturgeon, a graduate of Yale, as instructor. His nineteen years of service and its satisfactory fruits entitle him to rank among the great teachers of his time.

Commissary Bray of Maryland, through influential friends in England, gathered a school-fund whose benefactions overflowed into Pennsylvania on the North, and North Carolina on the South.

Meantime the Quakers, who had been the first, were always the most consistent in teaching the Negroes, often defying both sentiment and local laws that they might be true to their convictions. The Moravians also were active in the settlement at Bethlehem, Pa., as well as in New Jersey and in the Carolinas.

An interesting private venture was that of Mrs. Elize Lucas Pinckney, mother of the two patriot statesmen and soldiers of the Revolution, who, while managing her father's South Carolina estate, found time to teach a class of young Negroes to read. This about 1740.

Quite naturally, the American Revolution stimulated greatly the cause of education, both of the Whites and of the Negroes, when it was declared to be both the duty and the right of man under the new institutions. Washington, Franklin, Jefferson, and Madison, were foremost in commending gradual emancipation after education and training for citizenship. The following passages from Doctor Woodson's *Education of the Negro Prior to 1861*, fairly express the teaching of these and other Fathers of the Republic. "Many Americans who considered slavery an evil, had found no way out of the difficulty, when the alternative was to turn loose upon society so many uncivilized men without the ability to discharge the duties of citizenship." "These leaders recommended gradual emancipation for States having a large slave population, that those designated for freedom might first be instructed in the value and meaning of liberty to render them comfortable in the use of it."

How many of the heartaches and tragedies of the succeeding long years might have been prevented, had the people of America been as ready to follow their leaders in making pathways for peace and righteousness, and in establishing right and justice and self-government for their Negro and Indian people, as they had been ready to follow them in paths of war in fending their own rights and establishing their own self-government! But self-interest makes partisans of the general run of people not less now than then.

The Fathers of our Country, of our (then) new model of social life, found the motive of education to be comfort in freedom and usefulness in citizenship. They looked forward to the day when present slaves would be future citizens. They looked out upon their day in which education was the preparation of the embryo citizens. The thought of the era greatly stimulated interest in education.

In the northern States, education of the Whites took a leap forward; and not a few schools for Negroes, often separate at their own request, were opened and adapted to their needs and occupations.

In New England, Boston taking the lead, the negro children were generally admitted to the schools. The Negroes opened a school for themselves in one of their homes and applied for its admission and better equipment as a separate school, but this was declined.

The Clarkson Hall Schools in Philadelphia were the most successful, perhaps of the time; and by 1815 were offering free tuition to more than 300 pupils. Evening sessions were opened for adults. In Maryland, the Roman Catholics and Quakers were foremost in this field of endeavor. In Virginia, the cities of Alexandria, Richmond, Petersburg, and Norfolk were chief centers of education. In Alexandria, both races attended the same schools, a practice probably growing out of a like custom in Sunday school. In the rural districts, the instruction of the Negroes was done through the churches very generally, spelling and reading of the Bible being the goal.

North Carolina was even more liberal in her attitude toward education, and the Negroes "attained rank among the most enlightened in ante-bellum days." A remarkable instance, all the more so because the only one known, is that of the Rev. John Chavis, a Presbyterian minister, described as a full-blooded Negro of dark brown color, whose intellectual gifts early attracted the attention of his white neighbors of Oxford, N. C. He was sent to Princeton to see if a Negro would take a collegiate education. There he took high rank as a good Latin, and a fair Greek scholar. Upon graduation, he spent many years as a missionary and pastor until laws were passed, in 1831, forbidding Negroes to preach. He then became a teacher, opening a classical school for white pupils. Some of the most distinguished men of the State were his patrons and pupils. Professor Basset of Trinity College, N. C., tells his story, and names among his pupils, W. P. Mangum, afterwards U. S. Senator; Archibald and John Henderson, sons of the Chief Justice; Charles Manley, afterwards Governor of North Carolina; and Dr. James L. Wortham, of Oxford.

Beyond the parish school instruction, there were no schools reported in South Carolina outside of Charleston. In that city, schools for the free Negroes taught by white teachers were maintained up to the Civil War, and, indeed, until about ten years ago, when the Negroes requested their own teachers to be substituted for the Whites.

The combined result of the Abolition movement and the insurrections in 1830 and later, was a reaction against such education, very general over the entire country. Even in New Hampshire and Connecticut, attempts to open schools for Negroes were thwarted. Prudence Crandall, a Quakeress, was imprisoned in Connecticut; and a newly built school in Canaan, N. H., was wrecked. By about 1850, hostility had abated, and, in the North, activities were revived and stimulated; while in the South, Negroes, in small numbers, received some teaching in private or clandestinely. There were exceptions to this last statement, for there were open schools in Petersburg, Va., and in Charleston, S. C., as well as in North Carolina.

Before the Civil War, there were three opportunities for higher learning opened to the Negroes—Oberlin College, 1833, and Wilberforce, 1856 (both in Ohio), and Lincoln University, 1854, in Pennsylvania. Apart from these, a very few Negroes, as in the case of the Rev. John Chavis, were by favor admitted to other colleges in the North and West. The Episcopal Church was first in the field of education as of evangelization, the two were wedded together; but it was not until after Emancipation that higher education was made a part of her school system for the Negroes.

It is well to remember that, from our present point of view, the era we have been reviewing is a primitive one. Up to 1860,

Most of our population lived isolated, rural lives, and about one-half of our white citizens were deprived of schooling, and were classed as illiterate. Literary ambition was not a normal asset. Among the Negroes, but a bare ten per cent were literate at the close of this period; and, of these, the far greater number were free Negroes in the upper tier of States. During the Civil War, this percentage seems to have declined; and, at its close, something like six to eight per cent expresses the ratio of the literate.

The after-war period opens with the operations of the Freedmen's Bureau, created in connection with the War Department, to instruct and prepare the Negroes for the exercise of the rights and duties of citizenship. In this, the Government acted in conjunction with Boards of Churches, either already formed or at once organized.

In the South, the Episcopal Church and the Roman Catholic were the only large and undivided bodies with which such alliance could be made. The disaffection among the negro members of the Episcopal Church stripped her of any great powers of usefulness; therefore, the Boards acting with the Freedmen's Bureau were generally northern. Among these, the American Missionary Society, at first interdenominational and later Congregational, must hold distinction as first in service.

The most notable achievement of the movement was Hampton Institute, whose foundations were so wisely laid by General Armstrong. At once our Board of Missions organized a Freedman's Bureau; and through its co-operation there were opened, by 1870, a score or more of schools in North and South Carolina, Virginia, Tennessee, Georgia, and Kentucky. Of these, St. Augustine's, Raleigh, has had a continuous and distinguished career, the story of which appears later.

In 1873, the Petersburg School became a Normal School under Major Giles B. Cooke, a Confederate officer who, entering the ministry, became rector of St. Stephen's Church for Negroes. The story of this school is interesting as the model of other less noted ones throughout the South.

Early in 1866, our Church Freedman's Bureau sent, to Petersburg, Miss Amanda Aiken (whose memory has ever since been revered) as the teacher and organizer of St. James' School which was first opened in a private room. After many vicissitudes, the school was finally established in a house which, though inconvenient and distant a mile from the old site, served to shelter a good number of the 320 pupils formerly enrolled. Under the name, St. Stephen's, a new and attractive church and school were completed in 1868, and the Rev. Jos. S. Atwell, a colored priest, took charge the following year and conducted the parochial school until 1873. Then "Major Cooke," as he was generally called, already a teacher of the Negroes in the neighborhood, became rector. The greatest need of the time was for Negro teachers, hence the expansion into the Normal School. About as great a need was for ministers, and soon the Normal School added a course for their training under the Rev. Dr. Spencer, and became a branch of the Virginia Seminary. The "Major's School" became a recognized institution, gaining the complete confidence of both races in a day when such an achievement was not easy. Among the first pupils sent out was the Rev. J. H. M. Pollard, later Archdeacon of his native Diocese. The Rev. Jos. W. Cain had received his early schooling under Miss Aiken, and later was a deputy to General Convention from Texas. The Rev. James S. Russell was the first student of the Theological Training School, which laid the foundation for the Payne Divinity School. During its fourteen years of life, many were the teachers sent out by Major Cooke's School, and they were in great demand because of the excellence of their training.

One other type of school of this period (the type of many) should attract the interest of the student of the subject—i. e., the country schools. There is no better sample, perhaps, than the Clarkson School in Middle South Carolina on the Wateree River. The first Clarkson was an Englishman who settled in his Wateree home, east of Columbia, early in the last century. He at once built chapels on his plantations for his Negroes, and had them taught by a clergyman in catechetical schools. At his death, he left a substantial sum for this purpose; but the laws were adverse, and the bequest could not be fulfilled. It was to their honor that each generation should have desired to do more than compensate their Negroes for this loss. The last of the immediate family, Miss Julia Clarkson, is now the devoted teacher and lay missionary. The war and its aftermath were very destructive to the region, and the Chapel in Middleburg fell a victim, with other property. Only occasional Services could be held, and instruction was intermittent. The Rev. B. B. Babbitt, a graduate of Amherst, with a spirit and zeal holier than a crusader, had left his New England home to make good the promises for the Negroes. He took orders and was a welcome helper and pastor to the Clarkson's Chapel whenever his duties in Columbia allowed.

It was not until 1879 that Mr. Thomas Clarkson, in middle life, was ordained. He served his entire ministry fulfilling the ancestral trust as pastor and teacher. He rebuilt the Middleburg Church largely with his own hands, and preached and taught until his death. His wife continued the school to her death; and, since then, the daughter. Both have also taken the duties of lay-reader as necessity required. Mrs. Clarkson moved the school to her home in the Sand Hills. Services and school being held under a great maple tree at first, or, when the weather required, in a farm house, until, through the kindness of the Rev. Dr. Saul of Philadelphia, a chapel was built and later a separate school house.

The ideal had been a boarding-industrial-school, for two obvious reasons which the terms suggest. Then another fire destroyed the Chapel; but again it was restored, largely by the Negro members, and renamed St. Thomas in memory of their beloved rector, Mr. Thomas Clarkson.

The transformation in the life of the neighborhood is strikingly described by Miss Clarkson. The moral tone appears immeasurably better, marriage relations far more constant, embarrassment of inquiry about the parentage of children immensely relieved as compared with the postwar period of retrogression, and families quiet and reverent at Chapel, and sending their children to school. "The school house is the center of community life, the clubs meet there, the Woman's Auxiliary, and other organizations. We have sociables, wedding receptions, sometimes dances, and, last January, a Golden Wedding!" Sewing and cooking are taught, the former during the summer, and, at present, the latter in Miss Clarkson's kitchen, there being no domestic science outfit. A small canning outfit serves the school and community, and is used to the limit in summer. A colored missionary, the Rev. J. C. Perry, now serves the mission, baptizes the babies, and administers the Holy Communion. Miss Clarkson is the tireless day-by-day minister to all needs of the needy.

This description is extended to the present. It is a fair sample of the rural schools—more than fifty—throughout the Fourth, or Sewanee, Province, some of them with long histories and some recently opened. Scarcely one of the older schools but illustrates some motive of devotion on the part of white churchmen toward their Negro friends; and most of the later ones illustrate equally the zeal and self-sacrifice of more fortunate Negroes for their less favored brethren. The story of each is a tempting romance of missions, into which lack of space forbids our entrance in this study.

There were in 1922 fourteen such parochial schools in the Diocese of South Carolina with an enrollment of over 1,000 children, and in North and East Carolina there were twenty-one similar schools. These schools furnish the bulk of the students who attend such institutions as St. Paul's, Lawrenceville, and St. Augustine's, Raleigh. Many of them give courses in cooking, sewing, and manual training, with rudiments of a good high-school education.

In any discussion of the education of the Negro is involved naturally the all-important question, what is the purpose of his education? It has already been mentioned that a general prejudice against higher education existed, because of the fear that an educated Negro might be a trouble-maker. The weak points in much of the education of the Reconstruction period have also been noted. But present-day conditions have brought the education of the Negro prominently to the fore among our national problems as we realize what it means to the nation to have within its heart not only a race within a race, but an illiterate race within an educated democracy.

Feeling that the Church held the only satisfactory answer to this question, in that the purpose of education in the Church is to train mind and soul and body for a Christian citizenship, the idea of a Church Institute was suggested in 1905, and its incorporation was strongly and successfully advocated by Bishop Greer and Mr. George Foster Peabody of New York. This proposal was approved by the Board of Missions, and, in 1906, the Institute began its work. The Rev. Samuel H. Bishop, as General Agent, was the happy choice of the Corporation. He immediately made a thorough survey of the educational system of the South, and a second, equally thorough, of the work of the Church in educating the Negroes. The ultimate purpose was to be of assistance to all the schools in the Dioceses, but it was necessary for the new Institute to walk before it could run. The South was doing much, though with inadequate resources, and the North had become somewhat apathetic because of the many independent appeals by individuals with no organizations behind, or authority over, them. Confidence had to be restored in order that interest might be awakened. So the Institute was virtually an authorized medium of good faith between the Northern helper and the Southern school worker.

It was expected that this special organization would tend to emphasize the obligation of the Church for the moral and spiritual advancement of the Negro together with his intellectual advance. Its purpose was to give unity to the educational work already being done by the Church among the Negroes, and to make clear the great need of extension and thorough organization. The intention was that it should come to the relief of every Southern Diocese by developing in each at least one Industrial High School for the Christian training of teachers and leaders of the Negro race.

The founding of the Institute was to many a doubtful venture since it began its career without an endowment, and with an exceedingly limited list of subscribers; but the faith of its founders has been justified. In 1906, only three schools, St. Paul's, St. Augustine's, and the Bishop Payne Divinity School, accepted the supervision of the Institute. Today there are ten schools affiliated with it, with an annual enrollment of from 2,700 to 3,000 students.

The three largest and best defined of our schools—St. Augustine's, Raleigh, N. C., St. Paul's, Lawrenceville, and Bishop Payne Divinity School, Petersburg, Virginia—were chosen as institutions out of which "to create typical examples of successful correlation and development," as Mr. Bishop advised. These represented respectively a high degree of industrial excellence, advanced collegiate standards, and thorough training for the ministry. The first two furnished models for future Institute Schools in every needed feature of education. The Payne Divinity School should furnish all that the Church will need, for many generations, in its special sphere.

St. Augustine's, Raleigh, N. C., the oldest, owed its birth to the Church Freedman's Bureau. It was incorporated in 1867, and opened its doors in 1868, the Rev. J. B. Smith, D. D., being Principal. As soon as the Civil War was over, the need for teachers to instruct the millions of freedmen was recognized, and this was St. Augustine's first motive. As in the case of Major Cooke's School in Virginia, the need for clergymen was felt in North Carolina, and a theological department was opened about 1875. Here were trained such excellent men as Alston, McDuffey, Perry and Delany.

From the beginning, the collegiate department has been emphasized, and it now has no superior among the schools for Negroes in the South. All departments, however, are allied with the industrial and mechanical. Several of the school buildings are testimonials of the skill and industry of the students in carpentry and masonry, and there is abundant witness to that of the young women in the furnishing of rooms, hospital, and chapel, and in the making of their own clothing. There are 110 acres occupied by the school, affording both recreational grounds and agricultural training in intensive farming. St. Agnes' Hospital, founded in 1896 on the school grounds, has long established its reputation both for its benefits to school and community and as a training school for nurses. From sixty to eighty patients from the two Carolinas are generally in the wards, and thirty nurses continually under training in a three years' course.[1]

The fruits of St. Augustine's have gone forth to nourish the Negroes of every State beyond the seas and in every profession. Clergymen, trained in this school, have laid the foundations of Negro parishes and missions everywhere. Teachers, like Alfred Griffin, Professor Atkins of the A. M. E. Zion Church, Wm. A. Perry of our St. Athanasius' School, are everywhere multiplying the influence of their Alma Mater in geometrical ratio. Young men and women of St. Augustine's, wherever met, are holding up the high standard which made them what they are. Physicians, like young Delany of Raleigh (son of Bishop Delany), nurses, teachers, etc., have gone forth steadily from the student-body grown from the three of twenty years ago to the nearly five hundred of today.

St. Paul's Normal and Industrial School at Lawrenceville, Va., was founded in 1888 by the Rev. James S. Russell, now familiarly known to the whole Church as "Archdeacon Russell."[2] Confidence was soon established, the school increased, and in 1888, the Rev. Dr. Saul, of Philadelphia, furnished a building adequate for the needs of the time. Mr. Russell's ideals enlarged with the progress of his work. Property was secured upon other people's trust in the integrity of the hard-working young clergyman; for there was no money as yet, only faith. Gradual extensions were made, industries were introduced, buildings were erected by the pupils, and the farm was made productive.

Today the school has 1,600 acres and 40 buildings, large and small, three of which are permanent brick structures. The brick and much of the lumber are products of the school's lands and student-labor. There are fifty officers and teachers, and quite 500 pupils from twenty-six States, as well as from Cuba, Porto Rico, Haiti, Jamaica, and even Africa. Fully one-fifth of the negro clergy have been its students. It has sent out 600 graduates, and given training to 5,000 other undergraduates.

Doctor Frissell said of Brunswick County that St. Paul's School "has well-nigh revolutionized it." Literacy has risen from 12 per cent to 75 per cent. Moral standards have advanced, and the jail is deserted. Industrial standards share the impetus, and negro farmers occupy their own homes in great numbers in the two contiguous counties. County school houses have been improved, the sessions lengthened, and local self-taxation enlarged; while new schools have risen to meet the increased demand. The missionary spirit of St. Paul's is strong in its students. Numerous are the chapels and schools which owe their existence to its graduates. Doctor Frissell's judgment is more than justified.

The Bishop Payne Divinity School at Petersburg, Va., incorporated in 1884, "had its origin in the necessities of the case," as its catalogue announces. It grew out of the theological department of Major Cooke's St. Stephen's Normal School. Doctor Spencer, the first teacher, was appointed and supported by the Trustees of the Virginia Seminary. The school is finely located and has five good buildings, including a beautiful chapel recently completed, and maintains the same standard that other such schools have attained. The late Rev. C. Braxton Bryan, D. D., member of an old and distinguished Virginia family, was its Dean from the beginning. Examining chaplains find the graduates fully up to those from any of our Seminaries. The happy combination of able white professors with the splendidly trained and equipped Negro warden, the Rev. Samuel W. Grice, and the close association between the faculty and the students, make an ideal atmosphere for the highest and holiest results. The students have further training in life-work through their missionary activities in and around Petersburg.

Statistics of the school show that 92 students prepared there have been ordained to our Ministry; 16 of these have died in Orders; 76 of the Alumni are now in Orders. If you will add the two latter figures, you will find that every one of the ninety-two men prepared at Payne Divinity is honorably accounted for. Not one has, so far, put his hand to the plow and turned backward. These statistics do not take account of a considerable number who studied at the school, but for one reason or another were not ordained. The ten students this year in attendance are from ten Dioceses. Of these "three students served in France during the war, two of them were Lieutenants in the Army, one was in the Navy.... Two of our Alumni have been elected to the Episcopate, the Rev. James S. Russell, D. D., of St. Paul's School, Lawrenceville, and the Rev. Samuel W. Grice, B. D., Warden. Both declined the honor in order to continue their work in these important schools." Who will undertake to measure the value of the investment in human life represented in the Bishop Payne Divinity School?

By 1910, the strong, wise direction of the Rev. Mr. Bishop had so impressed the Church and made friends for the great cause which he advocated, that the American Church Institute felt itself strong enough to add three other schools to those under its patronage. Concerning them, Mr. Bishop wrote as follows in announcing their acceptance: "They are located in Georgia, Alabama, and Mississippi, where the need of effective work by our Church is greatest; and, notwithstanding pitifully small resources, they have done work of which the Church may well be proud." We review them briefly.

St. Athanasius', Brunswick, Ga., began its existence as a parochial school in 1884. In 1889, it was made a diocesan school. In 1910 a charter was obtained, and St. Athanasius' became a Church Institute School. Mr. William Augustus Perry, son of the rector of St. Mark's Church, Tarboro, N. C., and a teacher in his father's school, was called to be Principal. Mr. Perry is a graduate of St. Augustine's, Raleigh, and a B. A. of Yale

University. His purpose for the school was unconsciously expressed in this extract from a letter to Mr. Bishop: "I find myself arriving nearer and nearer to the conclusion that all unhappiness, all failures, all sins, are the result of ignorance somewhere—ignorance of self, ignorance of other people, ignorance of nature, ignorance of God. My people are accused of general incompetency, lack of skill, lack of finish; and to a certain degree, justly so. The cause of it all is that we do not get the thoroughness of preparation which we ought to have, and too much is expected of us with such poor fundamental training.... The standards are not too high nor the pace too great *per se*. What we want, what we need, and what we must have, is more system, more definiteness, and greater thoroughness in our early training.... If we get, in our youth, the thoroughness of training which the Church can give, we will shake off the stigma of inefficiency and superficiality." This has been his consistent effort throughout his eleven years of administration, and with marked success, as a visit to the school reveals.

The growth has been steady; and the attendance here, as in every one of our schools, fully taxes the capacity of the buildings. Industries are taught to both boys and girls, which minister to the needs of the community. The daily chapel, with instruction and lectures, make the spirit of the school-family.

St. Mark's School, Birmingham, Ala., was opened about twenty-six years ago in a rented room, with eight pupils. A lay-reader, C. V. Augustine, was teacher, and the mission was directed by the Rev. J. A. Van Hoose, of Alabama, a perpetual deacon whose enthusiasm and earnestness and great business ability have been the chief assets of the growing enterprise. A handsome building, now very valuable, is the present home of the school. During these years, the Negroes have contributed over $25,000 in fees and otherwise to its operation. In its curriculum, the school correlates literary, industrial, and religious education. The story of its graduates, too long to tell here, forms an interesting exhibit of splendid influence traveling to remotest country neighborhoods as well as to city homes and shops and offices. Plans for the enlargement of the scope of the work are in the making. The Rev. C. W. Brooks, a native of Baltimore and, for twenty-two years,

Principal, is a graduate of Howard University and King Hall. He has devoted his entire life to this splendid school.

The Vicksburg Industrial School, Miss., began as a parochial school during Bishop Thompson's later years, under the two Middletons, father and son, who were successively rectors of St. Mary's, Vicksburg. A suitable property was bought in 1907, when the St. Mary's School became twice as large. Upon reorganization, its name was changed, and industries suited to community life were introduced. Archdeacon R. T. Middleton, a rare soul, gentle and strong and modest, was the pervading spirit whose influence, to the day of his death in August, 1921, was powerful over the two hundred and more young pupils who annually attended. Here, as everywhere, the school has won the confidence of both races, and its graduates are generally making good everywhere from the Gulf to the Lakes. The School has its own Principal, but the Rector of St. Mary's, now the Rev. S. A. Morgan, is also rector of the school, and in charge of religious instruction.

The Fort Valley High and Industrial School, Georgia, accepted by Bishop Nelson of Atlanta, and helped by the Institute in 1912, was finally incorporated as an Institute School in 1919. It had its beginnings some thirty years ago. Its new life upon its present broad foundations is the result of the consecrated wisdom of a Negro layman and his wife, Mr. and Mrs. H. A. Hunt. They are both thoroughly practical and constructive teachers, who know how to relate the theory of books to the practice of industry. Fort Valley is the strategic Negro school of Georgia, both because of its central location and because of its good plant and its unexcelled history of success. The Principal is an authority on the sort of education which Fort Valley illustrates as no other can in that neighborhood. His work is of high value in community and State, as through institutes and conferences he disseminates his tested and approved methods. It would be invidious to select any one avenue of excellence to illustrate the work of Fort Valley, where all attain so high an average. Thus guarded, it may be proper to say that the contribution to the rural schools made through graduates equipped to meet rural problems, alone justifies every dollar of annual expenditures.

In 1914, the Rev. Samuel H. Bishop, General Agent of the Institute, died. His genius as a constructive critic had worked

WONDERS IN THE IMPROVED STANDARD OF ALL THE SCHOOLS. THE REV. ROBERT W. PATTON, D. D., SUCCEEDED HIM, BRINGING TO THE TASK OTHER AND EQUALLY VALUABLE GIFTS, AND THE INSTITUTE HAS GONE STEADILY FORWARD IN BUILDING UPON THE NOW WELL-ESTABLISHED FOUNDATIONS.

HERETOFORE, THE ABSORBING PURPOSE OF THE INSTITUTE HAS BEEN TO ESTABLISH THE CHARACTER OF THE SCHOOLS; NOT SO MUCH TO PRODUCE UNIFORMITY AS TO ENCOURAGE AND TO STRENGTHEN THE INDIVIDUAL CHARACTERISTICS OF EACH, WHILE DEVELOPING AN "INSTITUTE CHARACTER" IN ALL ALIKE. THIS HAD BEEN WELL ACCOMPLISHED BY MR. BISHOP. THE INSTITUTE COULD NOW LOOK OUT WITH CONFIDENCE UPON THE MISSION OF THE SCHOOLS TO THE LIFE OF THEIR CONSTITUENCIES. THE SUPREME NEED OF THE TIME WAS, AND IS, FOR TEACHERS PROPERLY EQUIPPED AND WITH ADEQUATE DEVELOPMENT IN CHRISTIAN CHARACTER TO BE THE BUILDERS OF OTHERS. SO THE SCHOOLS HAVE BEEN IMPRESSED WITH THIS GREAT MOTIVE TO WHICH THE BROAD CULTURE OF CLASS-ROOM WORK, DOMESTIC TRADE, AND AGRICULTURAL TRAINING ALL CONTRIBUTE, TO THE GREAT ADVANTAGE OF THE TEACHER. THE WORD "TEACHER," AS HERE USED, COMPREHENDS ALL CALLINGS, FROM PULPIT TO FARM, THROUGH WHICH OTHERS MAY BE GUIDED. AT THE SAME TIME SPECIAL CARE IS TAKEN TO TRAIN TEACHERS, TECHNICALLY SO CALLED, FOR SERVICE IN SCHOOLS BOTH PUBLIC AND PRIVATE.

IN 1914, ST. PAUL'S SCHOOL, ATLANTA, WAS ADDED TO THE LIST OF INSTITUTE SCHOOLS. BUT IN 1916, A DISASTROUS FIRE CARRIED THE BUILDING AWAY, ALONG WITH MANY CITY BLOCKS.

IN 1920, THE OKOLONA INDUSTRIAL SCHOOL, MISSISSIPPI, AND THE GAUDET INDUSTRIAL SCHOOL NEAR NEW ORLEANS, APPLIED FOR ADMISSION AMONG THOSE UNDER THE CHURCH INSTITUTE. THE OKOLONA SCHOOL WAS ACCEPTED BY THE DIOCESE OF MISSISSIPPI AND BY THE INSTITUTE, AND BEGAN LIFE UNDER THE NEW RELATION, JANUARY 1, 1921. ITS FOUNDER AND STRONG ADMINISTRATOR EVER SINCE, IS PRESIDENT WALLACE A. BATTLE, ONE OF THE FOREMOST NEGROES OF HIS NATIVE AND ADOPTED STATES, ALABAMA AND LOUISIANA, A NEGRO OF THE NEGROES. HIS FATHER WAS A LANDOWNER, AND ON THE FARM YOUNG BATTLE WON THE TITLE, "THE HARDEST WORKER ON COWIKEE RIVER." HE ATTENDED TALLADEGA COLLEGE, ALABAMA; AND, STILL LATER, BEREA COLLEGE, KENTUCKY, WHERE HE GRADUATED, WITH THE B. A. DEGREE. SUMMER COURSES IN

AGRICULTURAL COLLEGES IN ILLINOIS, AND IN THE UNIVERSITY OF WISCONSIN, FURTHER FITTED HIM FOR HIS CHOSEN LIFE-WORK.

"IT WAS AT TALLADEGA," HE WROTE, "TEN YEARS BEFORE OKOLONA WAS FOUNDED THAT I RESOLVED THAT THERE WOULD BE AN INDUSTRIAL SCHOOL WITH HIGH STANDARDS IN THE MOST NEEDY STATE IN THE UNION, IF THE LORD WOULD GIVE ME STRENGTH TO FINISH. I KEPT MY VOW, AND OKOLONA IS THE RESULT." NOTHING HAS EVER BEEN ABLE TO TEMPT HIM FROM THIS CHILD OF HIS CONSECRATED LOVE. IN THE MOST LEAN AND TRYING YEARS, HE DECLINED THE PRESIDENCY OF ALCORN, THE STATE AGRICULTURAL COLLEGE FOR NEGROES, AND OTHER FLATTERING OFFERS. THROUGH ALL, AND FROM THE BEGINNING, AMONG WHITE FRIENDS, TWO STAND OUT AS UNFAILING SYMPATHIZERS—THE HON. BENJAMIN J. ABBOTT, AN OLD CONFEDERATE VETERAN, AFTER WHOM THE FIRST LARGE PERMANENT BUILDING IS NAMED; AND CAPT. A. T. STOVALL, A DISTINGUISHED LAWYER, AND SON OF ANOTHER OLD CONFEDERATE OFFICER. THERE WAS PREJUDICE TO BE OVERCOME AND THESE TWO WERE FRIENDS AT HOME TO KEEP WATCH AS FATHERS WHILE THE INFANT ENTERPRISE PROVED ITS RIGHT TO LIVE. A DISASTROUS FIRE SOON SWEPT AWAY THE FIRST BUILDING. CAPT. STOVALL SOUGHT HOME-AID TO REPLACE IT. PREJUDICE WAS NOT YET DEAD. APPROACHING A GROUP HE ASKED AID. QUICKLY THE RESPONSE CAME FROM ONE, A STAMMERER, "I WILL G-G-GIVE YOU A H-H-H-HUNDRED DOLLARS TO B-B-BLOW THE D——D THING UP." MANY RESPONDED IN BETTER KIND, THE BUILDING WAS RESTORED AND THE STAMMERING FRIEND, NOW A STAUNCH SUPPORTER AS EVERYBODY IS, TOLD THIS ANECDOTE ON HIMSELF AT THE LAST COMMENCEMENT WITH THE ANNOUNCEMENT THAT BATTLE'S SCHOOL HAD CONVERTED HIM COMPLETELY, AND THAT IT HAD NO WARMER FRIEND THAN HIMSELF.

THERE ARE FOUR HUNDRED ACRES OF FERTILE PRAIRIE LAND BORDERING THE TOWN, WHICH, WITH THE BUILDINGS, IS WORTH QUITE $180,000. THE FARM WAS THE BEST IN THE STATE DURING THE YEAR 1921. THE WORK DONE IS SIMILAR TO THAT AT FORT VALLEY. THE INDUSTRIES ARE ADAPTED TO ITS PRAIRIE HOME. ITS GRADUATES PREPARED FOR TEACHING ARE ACCORDED THE TEACHERS' CERTIFICATE OF THE STATE, AND PLACES ARE ALWAYS READY FOR THEM. MANY CHOOSE AGRICULTURAL AND INDUSTRIAL PURSUITS.

THE GAUDET NORMAL AND INDUSTRIAL SCHOOL, NAMED FOR ITS FOUNDER, WAS TENDERED TO BISHOP SESSUMS OF LOUISIANA, AND ACCEPTED BY THE DIOCESE AND BY THE CHURCH INSTITUTE, BETWEEN 1920 AND 1921. MRS. FRANCIS JOSEPH GAUDET WAS LED TO FOUND THE SCHOOL THROUGH THE TRAGEDIES WITNESSED IN HER LONG AND remarkable work in the interest of prison reform. Little children of her race, the offspring of criminals, were often committed to prison because the State had no other provision for them. Their morals were early corrupted in such surroundings. Mrs. Gaudet championed their cause, and the story of her fight for reform is one of the heroic romances of modern times. She brought the matter before the Prison Reform Association who represented her cause to the authorities.

"We cannot change conditions; we have no money," was the answer.

"I vowed," she said, "that I would build the home and school for these neglected ones if God would help me."

Shortly after this event, she was appointed to represent the Woman's Temperance Union in their International Convention at Edinburgh, Scotland. Hoping to further the cause of the Home and School, she accepted, mortgaged her home for the money needed for the journey, and set forth upon her double mission, determined to suffer any privations needful to fulfill her mission. After the close of the Convention, Lady Henry Somerset, President of the Temperance Union, kept Mrs. Gaudet busy upon a lecture tour in Europe for six months. She returned to New Orleans with about $1,000 towards the Home and School. Soon a suitable site was found upon the outskirts of the city, and a first payment made. The farm of 105 acres now has three main buildings, a barn and other small industrial houses, and a beautiful campus, shaded with pecans and adorned with shrubs.

"Through God's agents," wrote Mrs. Gaudet, "the buildings are furnished throughout, even to an ice pick. The whole plant is worth about $100,000. I place this plant in the hands of the Episcopal Church in the Diocese of Bishop Davis Sessums."

At present the classes run through the 8th grade. "We teach also domestic art, mattress making, chair caneing, practical truck farming under an experienced truck gardener, and the rudiments of carpentry. We have a well equipped blacksmith shop, but haven't the funds to supply a smith to teach the boys. We have at present (1922) eighty children, boys and girls, a majority of them orphans. I would give every child a good school education with manual training, and compel each to learn a trade, for I have observed in my travels through the State prisons that fully 90% of the prisoners have no trade. People who have trades are too busy earning a living to get in trouble."

Two other schools—St. Mary's, Columbia, S. C., and Hoffman-St. Mary's, Keeling, Tenn.—are assisted by the Church Institute, and will doubtless develop, in time, as have those here briefly described, when the forward movement of the Church fully reaches them. Of St. Mary's, Bishop Guerry writes: "Out of it is expected to come a diocesan school at the close of the Nation-Wide Campaign for the Church's Mission." Hoffman-St. Mary's has a rural setting ready to be developed in order that it may minister to the great Negro population in the Mississippi Valley of Tennessee. These are two golden opportunities for the Church.

In January, 1922, comes news of the adoption of St. Philip's School, San Antonio, Texas, by the Province of the Southwest, this being the only school for Negroes in that Province. Bishop Capers of West Texas writes: "I have asked the Church Institute to include this school within the selected number of Southern Negro schools that it fosters. The purpose of St. Philip's is to educate young Negro women in practical learning, domestic science, etc."

Every one of our schools, whether parochial or affiliated with the Institute, is crowded. With double the equipment the attendance would at once be doubled. There are nine million Negroes in the South. If an estimate may fairly be based upon the facts known regarding a half-dozen cities in two States, then quite one-fifth of the children have no room provided for them at all. If the overcrowded condition were relieved, another one-fifth would have to be provided for. The Church could quadruple its parochial-school equipment and still be unable to meet the demands.

In our Church Institute Schools, we are dealing with the smaller class who are able to go, some of them much beyond the common schools, and others to the College course, and still others to the University. From them must come the teachers, preachers and leaders. In most of our States, from twenty to thirty per cent of the teachers are not properly equipped. Here again, to supply the demand for good teachers alone, not to mention the ministers and other "learned professions," we should quadruple our present provisions. For we must remember that schools of the character of ours are few indeed. If this does not constitute a clear call to service, what indeed does?

FOOTNOTES:

[1] See Appendix, Note 1.

[2] See Appendix, Note 2.

Chapter VII
THE CHRISTIAN DEVELOPMENT OF THE NEGRO IN AMERICA

In approaching the evangelization of the Negro in America it is necessary to go back to the primitive days of the colonists in order to picture the scene at the beginning.

Whether in the villages or on the plantations, the large majority of slave-holders felt a genuine compassion and an honorable responsibility for the helpless human beings brought under their care. They felt also an equal helplessness in the higher realms of guidance of the people who must yet learn the language of common intercourse. The constantly increasing importations introduced a mass of unacclimated humanity which, as constantly, postponed the day of this common language and common intercourse. The America of today knows something of the difficulties attending a too rapid immigration. But this modern problem pales before that of the primitive era of the colonies, which, beset by the new problems of new surroundings, must yet meet those of their composite social life within. The slave-master looked out upon the Negro race, after a few years, in its varying stages from the newly-arrived slave to the domesticated servant, and saw manifest racial inferiority in every capacity through which he habitually measured worth.

The white settlers of America were distinctly Christian, though their religion was of widely differing brands. What were they to do as they faced the new problem of composite life? They did exactly that which was natural and normal to their varied religious principles. Those who were enough of Christians to realize religion as a paramount duty, at once began to associate the heathen Negro with their own Christian faith. At first, this was through the family or neighborhood services, prayer meetings, Sunday schools and the like. By and by, as life became more organized, churches were built, and the slave worshipped in his master's church, and was taught by his master's pastor. In many cases, the mistress and her daughters were his Sunday school teachers.

In time, plantation churches were erected primarily for the Negroes, though generally attended by the Whites.

In this natural way, the Whites sought to maintain and perpetuate their own Christian culture, and to impart it to their negro families in such measure as the latter could receive it. It was difficult enough at best, where preachers and teachers were few, and where the struggle for a firm foothold, in a new land, was apt to develop the selfish and the sordid in human nature. It was increasingly difficult as the age of the deists and agnostics grew older and more aggressive under foreign and American leadership. It had its baneful effect upon the Christianizing of the Negro in producing that inexcusable variety of agnosticism which declines to see God's image in His black children.

Thus naturally, yet under great difficulties, did the Christianizing of the Negro proceed until the last years of the seventeenth century, when recorded efforts become more frequent.

Prior to 1700, the Bishop of London, in charge of the Church of England in the Colonies, had attempted to supply the people with pastors, sending one or more commissaries; but these efforts had been only very partially successful.

Miss Helm, in *The Upward Path*, writes: "The first organized effort to give Gospel instruction to the Negroes in the American Colonies, was made in 1701 by the Society for the Propagation of the Gospel in Foreign Parts, a Church of England society, incorporated under William III. The first missionary, the Rev. Samuel Thomas, began work in South Carolina, where he and his successors met with 'the ready good will of the masters, though much discouragement was felt because of the difficulties of the task, not many of the Negroes understanding the English tongue.' The zeal of the Society and its missionaries increased, and in less than forty years the report was made of a 'great multitude of Indians and Negroes brought over to the Christian Faith' in different parts of the country; and, later, of a flourishing school at Charleston sending out annually about twenty young Negroes well instructed in English and the Christian Faith." Thus the work of the Church among the Negroes in America owes its organization to the S. P. G.

Before entering upon the missions of our own Church, a general view of the Christian efforts made will be helpful.

The reports made in 1724 to the English Bishops by the Virginia parish ministers, are evidence that a few free Negroes in the parishes were permitted to be baptized, and were received into the Church when they had been taught the Catechism. This statement is equally true of the slaves. And what is true of the Episcopal Church is equally true of the Presbyterian. In all cases, the earlier converts were members of the white Churches. Indeed, in the early days, separate churches for Negroes were never contemplated.

The Presbyterian mission was begun about 1747 at Hanover, Va., with immediate success. Other missions were established, and many godly men devoted their time to work among the slaves both in the towns and on the plantations. In the Carolina colonies the same zeal was manifested, though for the most part the members of this Church dwelt in the upper counties where slaves were not so numerous. This, however, presented the occasion of even closer religious relations. There are no accurate statistics of converts at hand.

A little later came the activities of the Baptists and the Methodists, which ultimately swept into their various folds the vast bulk of the race. The Baptists, under their policy in which each congregation is a Church in itself, established Negro churches in Georgia and Virginia as early as 1775. In 1793, the denomination, in its several branches, numbered about 18,000, and grew rapidly during the succeeding years. In 1860, there were about 400,000 Negro Baptists, not including children and adherents under instruction which would probably run the total to more than a million.

The Methodists began work with characteristic fervor about 1770, and some twenty years later counted more than 12,000 Negro members, all connected with the white congregations. In 1860 this number was increased to 207,776 or, including adherents, about a half million souls. The anti-slavery movements, which more and more estranged the Methodists, North and South, during the years 1820 to 1844, retarded for a time their work among the Negroes, but with the division, in 1844, into Northern and Southern denominations, renewed activity was attended with great success.

Dr. Phillips in his *American Slavery* says: "The Churches which had the greatest influence upon the Negroes were those which relied least upon ritual and most upon exhilaration." It is true that the straightness and suppression of form rigidly applied to a people whose chief mode of expressing both social and religious emotions had for centuries, been through dancing and folk songs, was a transition too radical and rapid to be widely accepted and absorbed; but certainly the forms of worship had their lessons. A wise use of both liturgical and extemporaneous services would probably have produced better results. The Methodists would probably have made *better* Christians, and the Episcopalians *more*, had each combined the methods of both.

When education in the South was prescribed, the free, unliturgical services undoubtedly influenced a far greater number than could be reached by any other means.

The moral training of the people was a matter of the most vital importance. Infractions there were unquestionably, many of them, and worse than no help from some of the Whites; but the Church's steady voice and practice were powerful aids to the Negroes, and no less powerful restraints to the Whites. Admixtures were common enough, and would doubtless have increased had the old régime held; but the vaster commingling which took place during the four years of war in the slave territory, was one of the tragedies of the war.

On plantations belonging to earnest Christians, the sanctity of the marriage and of family relations was emphasized. It was not the exception but the rule, in such families, that all marriages were properly solemnized; and, in the case of domestic servants, the mistress or her daughters arrayed the bride, and the pastor or plantation preacher officiated at the wedding in the church or in the "Big House" parlor.

Every law of Church and State was conformed to, and repeated efforts were made by the Church to have everybody thus conform.[3]

Pastoral relations were attended with their difficulties in the city missions. The Rev. Paul Trapier writes in 1850: "The minister has still to lament that he can come so little in contact, pastorally, with his people, owing to the peculiar nature of their employment in the week and on Sunday. He fain would urge upon owners the obligation of so arranging their domestic affairs as to afford to their servants more opportunity for attendance in the Lord's House and on the Lord's Day. He can seldom see them during the week unless they are sick, nor then except in cases where he feels at liberty to go into the yards of their owners for that purpose. It gives him pleasure, however, to say that, wherever he has so presumed, his reception has been respectful and kind, encouraging him to ask the same liberty more generally."

When one considers the conditions under which the missions among the Negroes had to grow, the results were far more due to the grace and mercy of God than to the wisdom of men. This is said, not in detraction of the devotion of the men and women of all denominations who, conforming to the conditions which perforce robbed them of their full half-share, wrought their best under them as co-partners with God.

There was the ever-recurring repression by suspicious politicians, who feared that religious freedom might break down the barriers which secured the abnormal social conditions of slavery, often resulting in suppression of the gathering of Negroes for any purpose. There was the bar of illiteracy, where knowledge without book-learning, in an era of books, was sought. There was the exaction of moral standards, with home conditions conducive to none but low ideals. There was the spiritual culture of the racial tree, with no expectation, for that era certainly, of its full fruit-bearing in racial pastors and leaders. There was the agnostic scientists and their satellites with the infallible dictum, "The Negro has no soul," to be grasped at by the selfish materialist as excuse both for declining religious culture and for abusive treatment of defenseless slaves. These, and more besides, made the conditions under which evangelization in the South was prosecuted. And in the North, for reasons both like and unlike these, there were the same repressions and far more of prejudice, driving the Negroes into independent organizations so soon as law and popular approval would permit.

Under these conditions, it would have been surprising indeed if a host of notable examples of godly leaders had arisen. Nevertheless, God did raise up examples, in every degree of advancement possible to them, as illustrations of what the Negro would be capable of under less fettered conditions.[4]

It is not easy to follow the growth of the work of the Episcopal Church, for it is amazing to see how indifferent our forefathers were, and we are, to the accuracy of record of activities. In the beginning of the eighteenth century, there seem to have been no records at all in many of the communities, beyond such a general statement as this: "I have continued to instruct the Negroes of two plantations, and from the good evidently derived from such labors I am induced to wish that I may be enabled to extend my efforts to a much larger number of the same people."

Mr. Bishop, late Secretary of the American Church Institute for Negroes, mentions seeing, in the register of the old Bruton Parish, thirty-three pages consecutively devoted to the entry of the baptisms of Negro servants and children, extending from 1746 to 1797, and containing 1122 names. Numerous were the reports made to the Bishop of London by the missionaries from the Mother Church, of the careful instruction of the servants, and of the care of the owners to bring them to baptism. There being no Bishops, of course confirmation was not in view. Both white and colored were admitted to the Holy Communion at the discretion of their rectors. What was true of Bruton Parish is more or less true of the parishes of the Colonies from Maryland to the Carolinas and Georgia.

Naturally the first separate congregations were formed in the northern Colonies. Dr. Bragg of Baltimore gives an interesting account of the organization, in 1791, of the first congregation of Negroes—St. Thomas' Parish, Philadelphia—and of other parishes elsewhere. The white Methodists of that city, objecting to the intermingling of the races in their Church of St. George's, set the Negroes apart. The latter withdrew in 1787, and formed a Benevolent Society of Negroes, which prospered. In 1791, the Society desiring to become a Church, bought a lot, erected a building which they called after St. Thomas, and, by an almost unanimous ballot, voted itself into the Episcopal Church upon three conditions named in their petition to Bishop White. These were: first, that they should be received as a body; secondly, that they should forever have local self-control; and thirdly, that one of their number should be chosen as lay-reader and, if found worthy, be regularly ordained as their minister. Bishop White accepted the conditions, and on July 17, 1794, St. Thomas' Church was formally opened for services. Absalom Jones was chosen for ordination, and ordained a deacon in 1795, and priest shortly after—the first Negro ordained in the Episcopal Church in America. Of Jones, Bishop White wrote upon the occasion of his death, "I do not record the event without a tender recollection of his eminent virtues, and of his pastoral fidelity."

In 1819, the Negro members of Trinity Parish, New York, under the leadership of Peter Williams and others, and with the consent of Bishop Hobart, united themselves in the new Negro Church of St. Philip. The following year, Williams was ordained, and became the first Negro rector in the Diocese. "There was a great educational need, and he was the man who led the successful movement for a Colored High School in those early days. When the parish was denied representation in the Diocesan Convention (the members) quietly elected as their representative to that body the Hon. John Jay of the white race who was their real and sympathetic representative until he had succeeded in reversing the policy."

In June, 1824, St. James' First African Church, Baltimore, was organized by the Rev. William Levington. On October 10, 1826, the corner-stone was laid, and on March 31, 1827, the congregation occupied their new church which was that day consecrated by Bishop Kemp. "It was a day of peculiar significance to the descendants of the African race for all times to come," writes Dr. Bragg, "for it was the first occasion anywhere in the South, where a local branch of any of the existing white Churches had been initiated among the people of the African race, with all the powers of self-government, as well as with an educated pastor, of the same race as the congregation." The young rector was ordained priest in Philadelphia in 1828 by Bishop White, and the parish was incorporated the following year.

That the association of free and slave Negroes did not move always in the paths of pleasantness, is illustrated by the opening of St. James' to both classes, over the objection of the free. The earnest young rector seems to have been amply strong to compose the objectors, and to inspire them with a sense of duty to their less fortunate fellow-members. Among the fruits of his short ministry were the Rev. William Douglass, and the Rev. Eli Worthington Stokes, the former the first Negro to be ordained in Maryland (1836) and the latter the first to be ordained in St. James' Church (1843).

In 1843 Christ Church for Negroes—the first colored church in New England—was organized in Providence, R. I., by the Rev. Mr. Crummell; and, in the following year, St. Luke's, New Haven, Conn., by the Rev. Mr. Stokes. It will be recalled that both of these devoted Negro priests later gave their lives as leaders of the Church in Liberia.

Chronologically, Calvary Church, Charleston, S. C., organized in 1849 by the Rev. Paul Trapier, was the next to be built especially for the Negroes, as also to relieve the congestion in the white churches of the city. Because of the law against the assemblage of Negroes alone, a few white members were enrolled and always in attendance. The building of the church was at once begun. An unsuccessful attempt was made to destroy the church under construction, Mr. Trapier calmly announcing to the mob, "You will tear it down only over my dead body." After a public meeting at which the full purpose was explained, the building progressed peacefully, and the good work has continued to this time. Calvary Church bore the relation to the churches in Charleston that would now be defined by the term, a City Mission.

About 1850, St. Matthews, Detroit, Mich., was established under the leadership of the Rev. William C. Munro. The anti-Negro sentiment soon operated to the closing of its doors. The wave passing, it was again revived; but lived only a few years. Yet during its brief career, it served one purpose of supreme worth, for here the Rev. Theodore Holley, later Bishop of Haiti, received part of his training, and here he was ordained.

These parochial establishments—probably the only ones in America founded on so ambitious a scale—together with St. Stephen's, Savannah, in 1856, represented the beginnings of the purely racial churches before the Civil War; the initiation, in most cases, of local self-government; and the models of those to come later.[5]

It would not be profitable to describe in detail the work of every Colony and Diocese in the period before Emancipation, where the sameness of method and result so inevitably blends with monotony. The work in South Carolina, completely illustrative of all, will serve as a sample, and others may be briefly summarized.

South Carolina illustrates, more completely than any other, the features of work employed by all the Southern States.[6] Happily, there is almost a continuous record from which to draw. The *Chronicles of St. Mark's Parish* is especially valuable as a source-book. From it we learn that from the beginning, so soon as the Negroes were taught the language, Christian instruction and Baptism followed, wherever agreeable to the Negroes. This was provided for by Article 107 of The Code of Laws. No question was raised during the Proprietary Government. When the Royal Government was established, the question was raised as to the propriety of such instructions of the slaves, but the law stood as reaffirmed by the Legislature of 1712.[7]

In 1764, the Rev. Levi Durand of St. John's Parish, baptized the first child recorded as born of Negro Christian parents. This marks the beginning of a new era for the race; for until Christian faith, the instinct of prayer, and the habit of belief, come to be the heritage of a people, making the atmosphere of life, it is not possible to begin to build the generations into the great Temple as true and tried living stones. True, such habit, such atmosphere, may become in time but the empty shell of life that is dead; this is the danger against which Christians have had always to guard. Where Christian faith is surrounded by heathen superstition, it is thrown upon guard, if the faith be true. Its guard is apt to become increasingly relaxed as the atmosphere which surrounds it is of its own making. But this latter is, none the less, the very condition of progress, where faith is truly alive. Hence it was only when the Christian Negroes could make the Christian conditions in which to rear their children, that the conversion of the race could be said to have begun. From that year, 1764, the Christians of a second generation increased with their numbers, and vastly contributed to the better and more wholesome conditions to which their new brethren came.[8]

That the disposition to evangelize the Negroes gained complete ascendency with the success of efforts, is attested by the report of the "Committee of the Religious Instruction of Colored Persons," published in *The Gospel Messenger* of May, 1838.[9]

"St. John's, Colleton. The preaching upon the plantations has been continued, with increasing evidence of the benefit resulting, both to master and servant, from this branch of duty. The interest of the master in the religious instruction of his slaves, may be known from the fact that, on most, if not all, of the plantations visited, but half the usual task is given on the days on which Divine Service is appointed to be held. During the summer, a class of 44 colored children was regularly taught (orally) for an hour every day, by members of the Rector's family."

By the middle of the century such reports are the rule; there were fewer rectors of distinctly white parishes than of distinctly Negro missions.

In 1849, Bishop Gadsden, after noting in his address to the Convention, thirteen visitations "having more especial reference to the class of servants," adds this comment: "In my visitations, nothing was more gratifying to behold than the chapels which have been erected on plantations at central points for the more especial accommodation of the blacks. There are now at least ten such chapels. May they be greatly multiplied, and the day not distant when each large plantation, or two or more smaller ones, united, shall have a Chaplain and daily services!"

In that year, of the 430 communicants in St. Philip's, Charleston, 138 were colored; in St. John's, Colleton, of the 456, the colored numbered 401. These relative proportions of numbers represent fairly two types of mixed congregations. In 1850, the proportion of communicants in the Diocese was 2751 white and 3168 Negro. In 1857, as though in answer to the fervent prayer of his predecessor, Bishop Davis reports to the Convention, "The whole number of persons confirmed since the last Convention is: white 245, colored 628. I have been endeavoring to collect statistics of our operations among the colored people, but they are yet imperfect. There are, in the Diocese, 45 Chapels and places of worship for the slaves. There are about 150 lay persons, male and female, engaged in giving to them catechetical instruction. There must be 150 congregations, and catechumens in proportion to these

CONGREGATIONS AND TO THE NUMBER OF TEACHERS. THIS IS AS NEAR AS I CAN NOW ASCERTAIN." WHAT AN ANSWER, IN SEVEN YEARS, TO BISHOP GADSDEN'S PRAYERS!

But the increase in baptisms far surpassed other growth, and more and more Christian parents were bringing their children to the front. In 1858, here are some figures: In old St. Philip's, Charleston, 1 colored adult baptized, 18 colored children, 27 white,—manifestly proportionate to the Christians of the two races. In St. Stephen's, where the Church is not as long established and Services are less frequent, adults baptized, 119 colored; children, 11 white, 13 colored. In All Saints, Waccamaw, Mr. Glennie, the pastor of the Negroes for so many years, reports 52 colored adults baptized; children, white 10, colored 186. In his postscript, Mr. Glennie wrote, "Divine services for the Negroes on 19 plantations, 614 times; largest class of Negro children 70, smallest 6."

Among the postscripts to the report of St. Philip's, Charleston, is this one: "In the amount of missionary contributions is included $150 from the colored members of St. Philip's (and a few of St. Michael's) for the support of an African teacher; also $75 from the Bible Class of the assistant minister, for St. Philip's Scholarship in the Cape Palmas Orphan Asylum." This is not an isolated instance of the contributions of both slave and free for Missions.

The Rev. Dr. Taylor, missionary to the Negroes of Bluffton, about the same time, furnishes this testimony to the eagerness of the little Sunday School scholars, which is very characteristic: "In the discharge of my duties, I found much to interest me; the children were for the most part attentive and disposed to learn. I was recently quite gratified in meeting with a gentleman who owned one of the plantations under my care; he informed me that the children were very anxious, when he went among them, to repeat hymns, etc., which I had taught them, and for this purpose would often follow him."

By 1860, Bishop Davis was practically blind, though he continued to discharge his duties almost until his death in 1871. His journal for 1860, read by his son, contains a succession of confirmations of White and Colored, more of the latter than the former. And then came frightful war and its aftermath, with results in church life much like those in the industrial life of the Negro.[10]

A typical picture of the religious work of this period is given in the words of Mrs. Essie Collins Mathews.

"High above the Waccamaw river, stands the Weston Chapel, beautifully located. Through the years, I see the picture. It is built of cypress, has fine stained-glass windows, and in every way is a house well suited to the worship of the Lord. Adjoining, are a thousand acres of rice, the rice-mill, and other buildings needed by the planter. Hundreds of slaves are at work in the fields. When the clock in the Chapel tower strikes the hour for Evening Prayer, the many slaves start for the Chapel, and it is soon well-filled. The master is a lay-reader, and appears in his snowy vestments, and begins the Service we all love so dearly—'The Lord is in His holy temple; let all the earth keep silence before Him.' Then comes the General Confession, and the people drop on their knees. Do you not see them? Many are devoutly kneeling, the women with bright-colored kerchiefs on their heads and the men with their heads bared. The soft sunlight shines through the stained-glass windows and fills the Chapel with beautiful colors. The mocking-birds are singing softly in the live-oak trees just outside. The air is filled with the fragrance of the yellow jasmine, while the master joins with his black people in the prayer, 'Almighty and most merciful Father, we have erred and strayed from Thy ways like lost sheep.' At the close of the Service they sing, as only Negroes can sing, and with that quality of tone none others have:

'Through the day Thy love has spared us;

Hear us ere the hour of rest;

Through the silent watches guard us,

Let no foe our peace molest.

Jesus, Thou our guardian be.

Sweet it is to trust in Thee.'

They pass out of the Chapel silently, with a smile and a kind word for each from the master who is at the door to say 'Good night.'"

"The picture passes from our sight, and the words of the hymn can no longer be heard. We turn to the Chapel as it is today. Most of those old slaves now lie in the graves near by; and the good master, in the parish church-yard not far away."[11]

With this example in detail, it may suffice to say that, before the war, a like activity characterized every Diocese of the South Atlantic and Gulf States, including Tennessee and Arkansas, and to a less extent Kentucky and Texas where slavery was not prevalent. There were none without plantation churches, and few parishes without Negro members, and Sunday Schools for the children.

Such were some of the results of the labors of the early white missionaries. It is needless to add that no such results could have accrued had not the Negro himself possessed qualities out of which character may be built.

At the close of the Civil War, with one consent, the Dioceses of the South set themselves the task of building upon the reduced foundations. No one dreamed of a *laissez faire* policy. The leader spoke, and the Church, with reduced resources, responded. Some of the Bishops thought the old machinery sufficient for the new day; but most people recognized that the birth of the new era meant the change of the old order. The Negroes themselves had spoken by their actions, in refusing any longer to attend the white man's services. Plainly this indicated a desire for churches of their own, with local self-government such as had already been found palatable in political life. More or less of separation for the races in church had to be made, and more and more as time passed.

Gradually, as means could be provided, separate parishes were organized in the larger cities, beginning with St. Mark's Parish, Charleston, in 1866. At first, white rectors were the rule south of Baltimore. Occasionally, as was true of the pre-war period in South Carolina, Negro lay-readers were licensed; but plainly, and quite naturally, the Negroes wanted their own pastors from their own people.

From the establishment of the first Negro Church in Philadelphia, in 1791, among the free Negroes, the consistently prevailing demand of the freedmen has been for churches and pastors of their own. They first demanded this, and themselves suggested it to their white Bishops. Practically all of the Bishops met this desire with sympathy, Bishops Atkinson and Howe being foremost in meeting this natural ambition of the Negroes.

In 1873, Bishop Howe thus addressed his Convention: "Let a Missionary jurisdiction be erected by the General Convention with express reference to these people, and let a Missionary Bishop be consecrated, who shall give his whole time and thought to this work; who, as the executive, not of a single Diocese but of the entire Church, shall organize congregations, provide them with Church schools and pastors, and in due time raise up from among the colored people themselves, and to minister to themselves, deacons and priests who shall be educated men, and competent to the work of the ministry, and I cannot but think good would result."

The germ of this suggestion had been already discussed. The Methodist and Baptist Churches had been divided on racial lines, Negro Churches being provided; but the Episcopal Church had no such easy solution. The question was, rather, how to secure, without a division, what the Negroes manifestly desired. The General Convention of 1874, in its capacity as the Board of Missions, rejected the proposal of Bishop Howe. Its acceptance might have saved long years of controversy and vacillation—controversy over Negro suffrage in its Councils—vacillation of opinions, Negroes first asking separation for greater freedom in self-government, then demanding equal representation in Council; Whites first fearful of separation, then demanding separation in Council.

Meanwhile, the separate organization of Methodist and Baptist Churches, with freer worship and complete self-government, attracted and held most of the Episcopalians who had wandered from the fold, while others conformed to the Reformed Episcopal Church about 1874 to 1875. To this day, the pride of the Negroes in the "Great Negro Churches" with their own Bishops in the case of the Methodists, and, in the case of both Methodists and Baptists, their own strong leaders utterly independent of a responsibility shared by the

WHITE RACE, IS A POWERFUL MOTIVE IN HOLDING THEM TO THESE CHURCHES. THIS VERY GREAT ACHIEVEMENT WHICH THEY HAVE ACCOMPLISHED FOR THEMSELVES THROUGH SACRIFICES THAT WHITE PEOPLE OF THE SAME AGE KNOW ONLY FAINTLY, IS A SOURCE OF UNENDING SATISFACTION TO THEM, AND AN EVIDENCE OF THEIR ABILITY TO INAUGURATE AND MAINTAIN GREAT ENTERPRISES. THEY FEEL THIS PROFOUNDLY, AND ARE DRAWN, WITH THE CORDS OF LOYALTY, TO THAT WHICH IS THEIR VERY OWN, UNSHARED BY OTHERS.

THE MODERN ERA OF CHURCH ACTIVITY IN THE SOUTH FOLLOWS THE RECONSTRUCTION ERA, BEGINNING ABOUT 1880. IT IS, HOWEVER, ABOUT THIS SAME DATE THAT THE LARGER ACTIVITIES IN THE NORTH ALSO BEGAN.

IN THE NORTH, WHERE THE NEGROES WERE COMPARATIVELY FEW, SOME BECAME MEMBERS OF WHITE PARISHES. PERHAPS AN EQUAL NUMBER WERE GATHERED IN THE SIX CHURCHES BUILT ESPECIALLY FOR THEM PRIOR TO THE CIVIL WAR. OF THESE SIX, HOWEVER, TWO BECAME EXTINCT VERY QUICKLY—CHRIST CHURCH, PROVIDENCE, R. I., AND ST. MATTHEW'S, DETROIT, MICH. AND THIS WAS THE CONDITION UP TO 1880, SAVE THAT THE NEGRO MEMBERS OF WHITE AND NEGRO PARISHES INCREASED SOMEWHAT IN THE LARGER CITIES.

IN THE SOUTH, BEFORE THE WAR, FROM MARYLAND DOWNWARD AND WESTWARD, ONLY THREE PARISHES WERE ESTABLISHED FOR THE NEGROES—ST. JAMES', BALTIMORE; CALVARY, CHARLESTON; ST. STEPHEN'S, SAVANNAH—ALL WITH UNBROKEN HISTORY TO THIS DAY. THERE WERE INNUMERABLE PARISHES IN RURAL COMMUNITIES, ABOUT FIFTY IN SOUTH CAROLINA ALONE. NEARLY EVERY PARISH ALSO HAD NEGRO MEMBERS WHO NUMBERED MANY THOUSANDS. AFTER THE WAR, THE WORK WAS A WRECK, AND THE MEMBERS OF THE WHOLE SOUTH WERE COUNTED ONLY IN HUNDREDS.

AND HERE, IN PARENTHESES, WE OF THE EPISCOPAL CHURCH SHOULD RECALL OUR LASTING GRATITUDE TO THE AMERICAN MISSIONARY SOCIETY OF THE CONGREGATIONAL CHURCH. DURING THE ERA OF RECONSTRUCTION, WHEN OUR CHURCH COULD DO WELL-NIGH NOTHING WITH AND FOR THE NEGRO, THAT SOCIETY, WITH HOLY PURPOSE AND WITH ONLY THE NATURAL MISTAKES OF A PEOPLE FEELING THEIR WAY TOWARD A NEW PROBLEM, AND AT INDESCRIBABLE PERSONAL SACRIFICE OF THE WORKERS, ESTABLISHED SCHOOLS, PREACHED THE GOSPEL, AND HELD HIGH THE LANTERN OF THE GOOD SHEPHERD BEFORE THE BEWILDERED EYES OF A HOPELESSLY CONFUSED RACE. THROUGH THEIR WORK CHIEFLY, WERE THE LEADERS OF THE ERA RAISED UP. HAMPTON WAS FOUNDED MAINLY UNDER THEIR AUSPICES, and, until now, has been administered under their able and devoted missionaries in complete Christian courtesy to other Churches. Schools were established by them from Hampton around to Fiske, and though the South was, from the first, suspicious of their influence, they have long since won the confidence and regard of every soul who knows them by their fruits.

If we should follow the unhappy controversies of the ten years beginning about 1873, there would be disclosed ample reason for the continued estrangement of the Negro from the Church. His membership in the Church was never questioned. This, with all of spiritual privilege, was always his right. But the vexed question of the franchise was an ecclesiastical as well as a political matter; and, as always, each side had its advocates and its opponents. To the Negro, the question of representation in Conventions became important, as affecting the standing of his membership in the Church. Until that question was settled, he stood aloof. Generally, save in South Carolina and Arkansas, his right to representation was accorded, though there was some little variety in practical adjustment. South Carolina established, in 1888, a separate Archdeaconry where voice and vote, and conference with the Bishop would be free.

There was also the question of the fitness of the Negro, so new from slavery, for the office of priest. Prior to 1865, only fourteen Negroes had been ordained to our ministry, and a large proportion of these had Liberia or Haiti as an objective. None had been ordained in any Diocese south of Maryland. It would have been a totally new thing, and the South looked upon it with skepticism. Here, again, however, there were two sides, with constant controversy, resulting in reluctance on the part of Negroes to apply for Holy Orders.

True, the conviction that only Negro clergy could shepherd the thousands of stray sheep back to the fold, and the consequent necessity of providing such clergy, early overcame the hesitation of the Bishops; but, even so, Standing Committees felt neither pressure as did their Bishops. Nevertheless, of the 27 clergy ordained from 1866 to 1880, there were seventeen ordained in the South, eight in the North, and two in the West. This small number, while serving to reassure the Negroes of their welcome to the ordained ministry, did not bring back the wanderers to the fold in large numbers.

It was through the earnest devotion of men like Jos. S. Atwell of Virginia, William H. Wilson of Nebraska, Henry L. Phillips of Pennsylvania, J. H. M. Pollard of Virginia, Thomas W. Cain of Texas, Cassius M. Mason of Missouri, William Cheshire of Tennessee, that the seeds of a later harvest were sown in this widely scattered vineyard. With perhaps one exception, these early ordinants were the direct fruits of our postwar schools described in another chapter. Through these schools, White and Black together set themselves the common task of supplying the native pastors for whom our people yearned. Ever since, the ministry has been recruited almost exclusively from St. Augustine's, Raleigh—sole survivor of the old training schools; and from St. Paul's, Lawrenceville, and later ones.

The decade from 1880 to 1890 yielded the largest proportionate increase of clergy in the history of the Church, most of whom were prepared by those older schools. Many of these became the founders of parishes or schools or both.[12] With the access of the strong, earnest men of the '80s, there came new life into the Church's ministry to the Negroes.

The Church Commission for Work among Colored People was created by General Convention in 1886. The next year, a report was published of the work in all the Southern Dioceses, as well as in those of Springfield, Kansas, Missouri and Nebraska, where first beginnings had been made. In most of them, the Bishops were those who had seen the well-nigh complete collapse of the work of the former period. The tone of their reports is in marked contrast with those of ten or twelve years before; nearly all of them describe plans that only buoyant hope could contemplate. The display is pitiful in view of the great number of missions thirty years earlier.

Alabama, Louisiana, Mississippi, Texas, and West Virginia report one mission each, a new beginning in each case on the ruined foundations of the past. Bishop Wilmer of Alabama wrote with new hope of the revived Good Shepherd, Mobile: "This is a work of good promise.... The school in connection with the Church, and taught by one of my deaconesses, is a success. We are beginning to connect with it an Industrial

School; also an Orphanage and Sisterhood." The latter were never realized, but the Church has persisted and two others added. The congregations in Texas had increased to four, and in Mississippi to five. Florida and North Carolina had been rather behind the South Atlantic Dioceses in the old days, with many members in white Churches, but with few separate chapels. Their reports showed a strong foundation for the new times.

Florida had established churches in the upper and older half of the State, and missions at strategic points all the way to Key West. There were more congregations in each of the two Florida Dioceses, in 1922, than there were in the whole State in 1887.

North Carolina had been divided in 1884. St. Augustine's School had done great work. The old Diocese reported thirteen organized churches with "several admirable openings if we could feel secure of the means for inaugurating and carrying on the work in these new fields." In East Carolina there were five colored congregations, which were sufficiently organized to have regular buildings of their own. In both Dioceses, a plan of work, including parochial schools, is clearly before the Bishops and their workers. In 1895, the District of Asheville was set off. In 1922, there were, in the whole State, 39 congregations—more than double the number in 1887.

Maryland had not yet been divided. There were eight churches reported. And now there are quite as many in each of the Dioceses, with great growth of numbers, especially in Baltimore and Washington City.

Kentucky, then undivided, had three churches, with schools at Louisville and at Henderson. Now Kentucky and Lexington have three each.

South Carolina is beginning to overcome the earlier overwhelming losses. There were eleven congregations, with parochial schools for three of them. These had grown, in 1922, to twenty-five, with thirteen schools.

Tennessee had five missions, with a school for the members of Emmanuel, Memphis. These have doubled.

Virginia, reporting also for Southern Virginia, numbers six congregations and fourteen schools. Since then, the

CHURCHES OF THE VIRGINIA DIOCESES HAVE GROWN TO FORTY-THREE, AND THE MEMBERS ALMOST PROPORTIONATELY.

IN GEORGIA, THE MISSION WORK WAS RECEIVING WONDERFUL IMPETUS FROM THE REV. A. J. P. DODGE, THE BENEFACTOR OF THE NEGRO WORK, RECENTLY COME TO THE COAST REGION.[13] IN 1887, THERE WERE SIX CONGREGATIONS, THE REMNANTS OF ONCE FLOURISHING MISSIONS. MR. DODGE PUSHED HIS WORK OUT TO COUNTY AFTER COUNTY, ABLY SECONDED BY THE REV. D. WATSON WINN. RUINED CHURCHES WERE RESTORED, AND NEW ONES BUILT; EXISTING SCHOOLS WERE STRENGTHENED, AND NEW ONES FOUNDED. IN MANY CASES, THEY DISCOVERED OLD MEMBERS OF THE CHURCH UPON WHOM TO BUILD THE YOUNGER GENERATION. GEORGIA HAS BEEN DIVIDED SINCE THEN, AND THE SIX CHURCHES OF THE OLD DIOCESE HAVE EXPANDED INTO SEVEN IN THE DIOCESE OF ATLANTA, AND FIFTEEN IN THE DIOCESE OF GEORGIA OF TODAY. INTO ALL OF THEM, THE DEVOTED SPIRIT OF DODGE IS BUILT.

ANOTHER REGION WHICH IS QUITE TYPICAL OF THE GROWTH DURING THIS MODERN PERIOD, DESERVES OUR STUDY IN SHORT DETAIL, I. E., NORTH CAROLINA, WITH ITS SEVERAL DIOCESES. HERE, AS EVERYWHERE, THE NEW LIFE GREW OUT OF THE MEMBERS OF THE OLD DORMANT FIRE WHICH STILL SMOULDERED. NEARLY EVERY CHURCH OF TODAY BEGAN WITH A FEW NEGROES WHO CLUNG FAITHFULLY, IN SPITE OF DESTRUCTION ALL AROUND THEM, TO THE WHITE PARISHES, REFUSING TO JOIN THE PURELY RACIAL CHURCHES AS THE VAST MAJORITY OF THEIR FELLOWS DID.

"ST. CYPRIAN'S, NEW BERN, AND ST. MARK'S, WILMINGTON, WERE THE RESULT OF THE CONSECRATED VISION OF BISHOP ATKINSON WHO SOUGHT TO PRESERVE TO THE CHURCH THE FRUIT OF HER ANTI-BELLUM LABORS." THE FORMER WAS ESTABLISHED IN 1866, AND WAS MINISTERED TO, FOR MANY YEARS, BY THE RECTORS OF THE PARISH CHURCH, IN WHICH THE FIRST MEMBERS OF ST. CYPRIAN'S WERE REARED. I QUOTE FROM A MANUSCRIPT STORY OF THE CHURCH AMONG THE NEGROES KINDLY FURNISHED BY BISHOP DARST AND THE EXECUTIVE SECRETARY OF EAST CAROLINA. "IT IS IMPOSSIBLE TO ESTIMATE THE VALUE OF THE INFLUENCE THIS SCHOOL HAS HAD UPON THE LIFE OF THE COLORED PEOPLE OF NEW BERN. IT WOULD BE HARD TO FIND A NATIVE NEW BERNIAN ABOVE 35 YEARS OF AGE WHO DID NOT AT SOME TIME ATTEND THIS SCHOOL." THE OLD LANDMARK DID ITS WORK, AND ITS SITE IS NOW THE PARISH PLAYGROUND, STILL SERVING USEFULLY. THE CHARACTER OF THE PARISH HAS GROWN IN GRACE, ALL ITS PRESENT MEMBERS having been trained in the Church and in the old "Red School." Its contributions to the Nation-Wide Campaign were $1000 in 1921.

St. Mark's, Wilmington, was founded by the Rev. C. O. Brady about 1872. The parish is distinguished as the mother of clergy. The Parish School, with domestic science, has been a perennial garden of Church growth.

The banner parish of the Eastern Diocese is St. Joseph's, Fayetteville, founded by the Rev. Dr. Huske and the colored members of the old parish. It also led the Negro churches of the South in the Nation-Wide Campaign to which it gave $1300 in 1920.

St. Luke's, Tarboro, was organized in 1872 by Dr. Cheshire, rector of the old parish of Calvary and father of the present Bishop of North Carolina. In 1881, the Rev. John W. Perry became rector. The parish grew, and a school was opened which has trained many good Churchmen and some teachers.

St. Michael's, Charlotte, owes its birth and early nurture to Bishop Cheshire who, when rector of St. Peter's, opened the mission for colored people. A school was opened, children were trained, parents followed them, the church was completed, and an excellent plant provided equipment for a working congregation. Four men were sent forth into the ministry.

Another parish—the combined work of white and colored priests—is St. John's, Edenton. Founded by the Rev. Dr. Drane, about 1880, the Mission was able to build its church in 1886. The parish school has sent out many successful pupils who have taken high stand in their vocations. Direct fruits of Edenton, the mother of the district, are the Negro parishes of St. Philip's, Elizabeth City; St. Paul's, Washington; and St. Mary's, Belhaven.

The story of these years of re-establishment in North Carolina is one of beautiful sympathy between white and Negro workers, each ready to build upon the foundation of the other. Since then, the same sympathetic co-operation has attended the extension of the missions. Bishop Delany has been the founder of more than half of the existing churches in what is now, under Bishop Cheshire, his Diocese. He was consecrated Bishop Suffragan of North Carolina on October 18th, 1918, and enjoys the complete confidence of his brethren of the South.

Arkansas had no report for the Commission in 1887. She had not yet risen from the ashes of destruction. The Bishop Suffragan, Dr. Demby, writes: "The history of the Church work among the Negroes of Arkansas is very meagre; in fact, there is nothing really reliable ... outside of certain families who were members before the Civil War, during which old relations were broken up, due to the horrors of the war and the new conditions."

Bishop Pierce and his family had opened St. Philip's, Little Rock, about 1890. Under successive archdeacons in Bishop Brown's day, missions had been begun in Fort Smith, Pine Bluff, New Port, Hot Springs, and Conway. Most of them were without any substantial foundation, nor had they the equipment with which to establish churches. However, ground had been broken when Bishop Winchester came in 1911. He at once saw that the problem was unlike that in other Dioceses to the eastward, where, very generally, a remnant of the old, well-trained members of the white congregations were the foundation of the missionary renaissance. So soon as the Canon on Suffragans was passed by General Convention, he proposed its application in Arkansas; and, in 1918, the Rev. Dr. Demby was elected and consecrated. He at once entered upon his task as apostle to his race. He had at first to overcome the natural feeling of insecurity which intermittent ministry had engendered.

One of the chief obstacles to foundation work in this new era, has been the uncertain income for support, resulting in long vacancies. The natural consequence has been to create in Negroes, interested in Holy Orders, the sort of skepticism which asks, "If I join you, what next? Am I to be left shepherdless and isolated in a Church without companionship?" The old policy of begging an income year by year made this very generally inevitable. To overcome that handicap is no easy task. There were many others. General Convention had issued a challenge to the faith of the Church. Arkansas was first to accept it in the name of the whole Church; and, in her material weakness, sent forth the call of faith to Bishop Demby to lead his people in the Trans-Mississippi Province.

Two years ago, Bishop Demby sent forth a review of the field, and a call to the Church to give him means to occupy it. Of Arkansas, he wrote: "There are seventy-five counties in the state; in six of them, there are more colored than white people; Crittendon, 71%; Phillips, 78%; Desha, 79%; Jefferson, 71%; St. Francis, 68%; Woodruff, 58%. In only three of them has work been begun, though there are missions in several of the counties of the interior. We have scarcely begun to enter the great "Black Belt" which is ready and ripe for the harvest. What we need is substantial help to do the work to which the Church has called and consecrated us."

The Bishop is facing the whole task as it relates to American life, just as his brother Bishop, Delany, is facing it on the Atlantic coast. "The Episcopal Church is facing the American race-problem bravely and courageously ... and, in harmony with the program of the Sociological Congress, is doing it rationally and in the spirit of Christianity. There is no question as to its attitude against peonage, lynching, riots, mob violence, and court injustices. The Bishops and priests of the Church are one against all wrongs to the Negroes or any other race unit." He sees the call of the Church to contribute, in the best and holiest way, to the harmony of American life. He finds in this the surest ground of that reassurance of his race without which efforts are futile.

Much more, there is, but this may suffice to exhibit the breadth of vision with which our negro Bishops are viewing their great task. They are both in the heart of the Negroes' home, east and west. As few men can, they know the problems and difficulties, the achievements and hopes.

Turning now to the northern and western Dioceses, we find a corresponding growth in the number of congregations, with far greater proportionate increase in members, and in self-supporting parishes. The building of new churches fairly well marks the progress of the diffusion of population. Before 1880, the Negroes of the North and West were few in number, and only about ten congregations in the States of Pennsylvania, New Jersey, New York, Connecticut, Rhode Island, Michigan, and California, had been formed. A gradual transfusion then began, most of which could, for a time, be cared for by the white and the existing negro parishes. From that date to 1890, ten more congregations were formed. This is from Dr. Bragg's *Manual of Afro-American Church Work*, dated 1910. "Since 1900, the period of greatest influx of population from the South, 45 congregations have been formed in 29 dioceses, North and West. The Church in the North and West has been quite as much alive to the duties and privileges of Negro work as has the South, to which the many millions are native."

The next development in the upper Diocese came in New Jersey, long after the first establishments. About 1860, St. Philip's, Newark (the first in the Diocese and the last before the Civil War) was founded. So the two Dioceses in that state were ready to meet the new people who began to flow northward in the '80s, when St. Augustine's, Camden, was founded in 1888, and St. Augustine's, Asbury Park, five years later. These became the vantage points from which the present ten parishes have been formed. Sometimes the initiative came from the white parish, as in the case of Epiphany, Orange, first opened by the Rev. Alexander Mann when rector of Grace Church.

In 1865, St. Philip's, Buffalo, was opened, and the western Diocese had a home for its limited Negro population. St. Thomas', Chicago, was founded in 1880, and is one of the largest parishes of the North Central States. In 1883, St. Michael's, Cairo, Illinois, was opened by the parish church, and the Rev. J. B. Williams, just ordered deacon, served as rector. The site was strategic, at the head of the vast population of the Mississippi Valley. In 1885, came St. Philip's, Omaha, Nebraska; and St. Simon's, Topeka, Kansas, which, with St. Augustine's, Kansas City, opened the near West for the later migrations. The next year, St. Augustine's, Boston, initiated the separate congregations in Massachusetts for the colored members of parishes which were becoming overcrowded. These were followed by missions in Southern Ohio, Delaware, Minnesota, Ohio, and Indianapolis, through the years to 1900. Thus the Negroes in their increasingly widespread movements found Church homes in nearly all of the centres to which they were being attracted.[14]

In the summer of 1921, *The Church Advocate* published a statement of comparative statistics of growth in the provinces. The figures, probably of 1920, from the entire Church, were, Clergy 155, Congregations 283, Communicants 30,113. The congregations now number 289, and probably the increase of clergy and members corresponds. Then follow these paragraphs: "In the year 1907, in the Southern States included in the Province of Sewanee, there were reported 5,719 colored communicants. Fourteen years later, 1921, within the same territory, there are reported 6,393 colored communicants, or a total gain in fourteen years of 674. In 1907, the New England States, New York, New Jersey, and Pennsylvania, reported in the aggregate 4,413 colored communicants. In 1921, this same group of States report 11,601 communicants, an increase, in that period, of 7,188."

These figures are probably very nearly accurate; and they suggest an inquiry to which no simple yet complete answer can be given. Two explanations stand out above others: first, that the reasons which have retarded the growth of the Episcopal Church in the South are the same for White and Black alike, i. e., its ultra-conservative character, involving an unconsciously aristocratic spirit which may often seem cold and forbidding. The second explanation may be found in the economic pull toward the busier North, drawing the most enterprising element of both races. From the ministry, through business circles, to the industrial trades, our northern centres have a large percentage of Southern life. This is especially and increasingly true of our Negro life during the years since 1900. The Episcopal Church is cultural to a marked degree; her Services not only encourage but impart culture. Her Negro members quickly become a desirable class. Thus the experience of Mississippi during the past twelve years may be somewhat exceptional, but it is still typical of the whole South. Had we held our increase through confirmations and through births in the Church, the number today would be more than trebled. In the one war-year of greatest migration, the colored congregations lost quite 50% of their numbers; these migrants are now to be found very generally in the churches all the way from Chicago to Boston.

It is sometimes very discouraging to our colored clergy to see a fine, sturdy nucleus of a strong parish evaporate in a few weeks. The loneliness of it is intense. All honor and profound respect for the men who hold their posts on a progressive picket-line, standing alone, sometimes, until recruits answer the call! They are at the training-stations, sending on the trained to the larger centres, North and South.

In the Government Report on Negro Migration, 1916-1917, Dr. James H. Dillard gives a striking illustration furnished by the reports of the Durham School, Philadelphia. "I thought that the new enrollment would probably afford some information as to new arrivals. The Principal had enrolled the new pupils on sheets containing fifty names, and had been careful to enter opposite each name the place from which the pupil had come. I took six sheets at random and found ... among the new pupils between forty and fifty per cent from the South."

The Church is one, and the one lesson of practical value from this recital is that the Church be ever watchful and ready in pastoral care of a flock wandering far from accustomed folds, and diligent to conserve the fruit of a common sacred task. With this as the over-mastering motive, the scouts on outpost duty will rejoice equally with the mobilized army in close array, that all stand steadfast to duty.

FOOTNOTES:

[3] For a full discussion of this matter, see the Report of a Committee of the Diocese of South Carolina, 1859.

[4] See Appendix, Note 4.

[5] See Appendix, Note 5.

[6] See Appendix, Note 6.

[7] See Appendix, Note 7.

[8] See Appendix, Note 8.

[9] For Resolutions contained in this Report, see Appendix, Note 9.

[10] See Appendix, Note 10.

[11] See Appendix, Note 11.

[12] See Appendix, Note 12.

[13] See Appendix, Note 13.

[14] See Appendix, Note 14.

Chapter VIII
What of the Future?

A young professor, after reading portions of the manuscript here printed, asked, "Where is this leading to? Suppose the Negro is evangelized and educated as thoroughly as your ideal for him seems to desire. What will happen, and what is to be his relation to the white people in this country?" That has been the white man's question ever since the possible consequences of his bringing the Negroes to the new land were brought home to him. The question was faced with impelling emphasis as the Fathers of the Republic contemplated the purposes and ideals of the new form of government which they established. From this government they expected to realize an equality of opportunity for all men such as no other had ever dreamed of as an ideal to be desired. The Declaration of Independence inevitably brought the white man's question to the fore as he faced the red man, owner by right of occupation, and the black man, now become American by right of birth. Just as inevitably, with the first freedman, arose the Negro's question, "What is my status in American life?" The clamor for a true, unclouded answer to both questions increased with the increasing numbers of the freedmen.

Even during the slave era, with the growth in numbers and in race consciousness on the part of the intelligent, educated few, the question of the status of the Negro in American life inevitably arose. Among those who were first to awake to the inevitable was the Rev. James W. C. Pennington, D.D., of New York, foremost among the Negro scholars and leaders of the last century.

Lecturing in England and Scotland about 1840, Dr. Pennington said, "The colored population of the United States have no destiny separate from that of the nation in which they are an integral part. Our destiny is bound up with that of America. Her ship is ours; her pilot is ours; her storms are ours; her calms are ours. If she breaks upon any rock, we break with her. If we, born in America, cannot live upon the same soil on terms of equality with the descendants of Scotchmen, Englishmen, Irishmen, Frenchmen, Germans,

Hungarians, Greeks, and Poles, then the fundamental theory of America fails and falls to the ground."

The same question is involved today in any discussion of the status of the Negro. The Negro cannot answer it alone, the white race must enter with him into these too often forbidden portals, and help him unlock the door of mystery.

What, then, is the Negro's status in American political life? It is that which our national Constitution gives him, with lawful qualifications made by several States. No sincere Christian can stand for the breaking or the ignoring of law. If laws are bad, change them; but safety, justice, and decency demand that they be obeyed—else, anarchy. The national Constitution declares the ideal. The qualifications of the States are based upon the same just principle "that the best qualified should rule;" the practice of the politicians is quite another thing. The wise know that the resort to illegality to gain ends is as the pit to destroy others.

During the slave era, the negro leaders of the freedmen set themselves to the task of establishing their citizenship; so that this question was a live issue even before the Civil War. Out of it, grew two distinct theories of relationship of the Negro to American life. Richard Allen was the leader of one school of thought. He and his confrères had been treated with scant courtesy in the white Methodist Church of Philadelphia; he therefore withdrew, and founded the African Methodist Episcopal Church. His contention was that the Negro should have his own Church, his own leaders, and should build his own enterprises in every line of endeavor.

The leader of the opposite school was Frederick Douglass, who thus declared the principle upon which his following proceeded: "I am well aware of the anti-Christian prejudices which have excluded many colored persons from white churches, and the consequent necessity of erecting their own places of worship. This evil I would charge upon its originators, and not the colored people. But such a necessity does not now exist to the extent of former years. There are societies where color is not regarded as a test of membership, and such places I deem more appropriate for colored persons than exclusive or isolated organizations."

While, in detail, these two theories may vary in their developing expression, the principles upon which they were founded remain, and powerfully affect the Negroes' attitude towards all the departments of our complex life. The question was both natural and inevitable, and became an increasingly live issue with the growing free population, as they looked forward hopefully, in 1850, to the day of universal freedom. It was a question which could not be answered by themselves alone. The disfranchisement of the Negro before the Civil War, was so nearly universal, that the answer to his question of relation to the political life of America was clearly a negative one. But there was a growing sentiment in the Northern States, coincident with the rise of the Abolition party, toward Negro suffrage on a restricted basis.

It is probable that President Lincoln's very conservative view of the matter would have expressed the view of the growing minority of whites before the war; and, had he lived after it, it is equally likely that it would have prevailed over all the reunited Union, as it does, with qualifications, in many States at the present time. I quote his letter, written in 1864, to the Governor of Louisiana, and printed in the *Negro Year Book* of 1919. "Now you are about to have a Convention which, among other things, will probably define the elective franchise. I barely suggest, for your private consideration, whether some of the colored people may not be let in, as for instance, the very intelligent, and especially those who have fought gallantly in our ranks. They would probably help, in some trying time to come, to keep the jewel of liberty in the family of freedom. But this is only a suggestion, not to the public, but to you alone." Again in his last public speech, April 11, 1865, in speaking of the new Louisiana Government, he said: "It is also unsatisfactory to some, that the elective franchise is not given to the colored man. I would myself prefer that it were conferred on the very intelligent, and on those who serve our cause as soldiers."

It is true that a State like Mississippi would be in an intolerable condition if unqualified suffrage were in practice, because the majority of the Negroes and some of the Whites are either illiterate, or too nearly so, to be intelligent voters. It is safe to say that no intelligent man, black or white, in the State, would vote for unrestricted franchise with its certain consequence of domination by the mass of the unfit.

In no sense does this age face the problems of the old reconstruction of 1865 to 1880. But the tragedies of that old time were not primarily of the Negro's making. The thoughtful, older men, who are familiar with the age, and analyze the motives of conduct, know that Negroes, whose loyalty to their old masters has never faltered, transferred that loyalty to their liberators in utmost good faith and profound gratitude. We know that the Negro bowed before the "Yankee" with the same motive of grateful reverence that the American bows to the statues of Washington and Lafayette. The wise, thoughtful Negro of today looks back upon that wild era, and sees the mistakes and the loss to his race; while he lets others do the talking. Its lessons are not lost to him, difficult as it is for many people in the South to believe it. No one can read between the lines of the lectures of their great leaders without knowing how keen their insight is. An illuminating example is Dr. Isaiah Montgomery's debate in the Mississippi Constitutional Convention in favor of the present suffrage law of the State.

There is but one demand—that laws be honestly administered. But this would involve office-holding! Well, why not if it contribute to mutual interest? Is it true democracy that would leave half of a population (as in some communities) unrepresented, all the way from State Legislature to policemen of a negro ward in town? Can that be Christian justice, whose approval we ask of our Lord, but which deprives a people of the right to guard the most sacred trust which God imposes—the homes in which they live? There are just as many classes among the Negroes as among the Whites. They are all forced into solidarity for like reasons that make the solid South. Neither is healthy. Both are based on unreasonable prejudice. The solid Negro believes he faces a solid white wall. The solid South believes it faces two solids, North and Negro. In neither case is it true. Just let somebody begin to do justly, trust the other fellow, and trust, above all, God's power to inject a sense of justice and fair play even where human shortsightedness cannot see, and most of our troubles in this line would evaporate. The problem of trust is at once a community problem and a world problem which only the determined faith which removes mountains can solve.

Every one of our States has some wise, patriotic Negro leaders who are earnestly studying the problems of race and of State, and who are profoundly anxious that race-integrity be maintained and race-relations be cordial and mutually helpful. They, and they alone, know the trials and burdens, the achievements and ambitions of their race so perfectly as to witness with authority. Over our entire nation, it is by the white race that the laws are made and executed, that social needs are ministered to, that prisons are administered, and that education is provided, and health and sanitation supervised. There is not a State in which the regulation of civic life would, or could, be turned over to the Negroes. This lays upon the Whites the chivalric obligation of studying, the more conscientiously and carefully, the needs and interests of their Negro fellow-citizens. This cannot be done apart from the highly intelligent Negroes. In our State governments we should have Negro representatives of their race to confer with law-makers as advisers. An hour's conference with two or three of their leaders, chosen for the purpose by their own people, informed and freely representing their interests, would clear the atmosphere of racial misunderstanding, as no debate of a white legislature could do in a whole session.

In our city administration, the white and colored population are, by mutual choice, not by law, segregated; yet, through employment in daily contact, if one member suffer, all members suffer with it—but the Negro, most. In many cities, never a peace-officer is seen, save *AFTER* crime has been committed. How much better that his ward of the city be guarded and cared for *BEFORE*, so that the order and decency which ordinarily prevails, in spite of neglect, may be guarded and maintained! The Negroes should have their own peace officers; and their right to protect their own homes should be kept utterly inviolate. Citizenship is a sacred trust, and the care of citizens and the harmony of life demand that the most wholesome conditions of life be made for all alike.

We, of the Episcopal Church, have tested this out through many years. We have sat in councils, in conferences, on committees and boards with Negroes. With scarcely an exception, we have found them as courteous as ourselves. In counsel, some are wise and valued advisers; some are less so; none are useless. Their addresses sound much like ours; upon matters of their own race, far more illuminating than ours, as a rule. We mutually fulfil the covenant which Dr.

Washington's Atlanta speech proposed, and which our whole people accepted in 1884. The substance of that proposal was that "in our outward, common life, in all that goes to make a harmonious relation and a prosperous people, we are a unit like a man's hand; in our inner social life, in all that contributes to racial integrity and the separate trusts that God imposes, we are separate as the fingers of that hand; but hand and fingers unite in striving to perfect the human family, to strengthen and build up, to guard and to purify, the great living Temple of God." Can the Church be God's Church, and stand for less?

The educated, intelligent Negroes of today, who read and think, are as anxious to contribute to the best interests of their communities, their States, and our common Nation, as are the Whites. This has been tested in community "clean-up campaigns," in anti-tuberculosis movements, in Liberty Loan drives, in volunteers for war, in active service in army and navy—in every movement in which they have been assigned a share. They have never asked exemption from any duty. If service be a badge of honor, the Negro has won it. If the laborer is worthy of his hire, then the Negro has earned the fruit of his service as a citizen. If there are difficulties to be encountered in the bestowal of his earnings, they should be met squarely. Conference on any vital subject whatever, is always courteous and cordial when the Negro is accorded the place that God gave him in creating him a man. That, too, is not conjecture, but long-proved fact. When men have learned that the house of State is as much God's house as that of Church, we shall learn how to hold brotherly conference with black or red or yellow or brown, and differences and misunderstandings and green-eyed hatred will be banished.

Utopia, one says! Possibly; but if there were no Utopia to strive for, we would cease the striving, and be content to live in any jungle that gave us birthplace.

The philosophy of life changes as present ideals are reached, and as loftier ones replace them in the half-conscious process of spiritual growth. A retrospect of child-growth, with its heightening ambitions urged upward by progressive ideals and mental and spiritual growth, illustrates this changing philosophy. It ought also to illustrate the folly of a rigid fixedness in life's relationships such as leaves no room for that expansion which enlightenment brings both to ourselves and to others. Thoughtful people cannot suppose that our ideas about race-relations will always remain just as they are. They have changed greatly in the past, and we do not know just how God is going to lead us through the maze of the future. There is but one sure rule—to do justly, and to know that righteous obedience to God's law of justice, and conformity to God's law of love, constitute the wisdom which will be justified of its children in never-ending generations. There ought also to be a human reliance that can be depended upon. In every age, it has been the unusual stability of character based upon profound religious conviction on the part of the few, that has saved the many.

We have traced, in brief, the lives of some of those outstanding Negro characters of deep conviction, who have been the ensigns of their people. It was upon these men of Church and School, with their co-workers like Booker Washington and others, that the duty of leadership has fallen in these years, beginning in the '80s, and continuing until now, when new relations between the races have been in the making. At the beginning of this period the old régime had not yet been forgotten; the bad start of Reconstruction had muddied the waters, and no one could see the bottom; the new freed race had still to try its wings; the old survivors of both races—now few, indeed—who had made the old relations, were then the many in middle life clinging to the past; the old "Uncles" and the old "Mammies" were still too many, and the endearment of the old ties was still too strong to give immediate place to a new relation between free Whites and black Freedmen or their free-born sons.

The North did not know just where to place the members of a race in its existing level of development; and the South was unwilling to have them where Reconstruction had placed them. In consequence that happened, which has always happened in the history of the race when others had the power; the Negroes were largely unconsidered or ill-considered, and their real interest and their best good were alike submerged, while North and South spent weary years in controversies in which each side was sure of its own rectitude and distrustful of the other's. No better condition for missing the conservative right can be found than that which extremist advocates necessarily make in imputing error to others because of the conviction that those others must think wrong. Through such a maze, the younger leaders were raised up to guide their people, and to demonstrate to the older, more advanced, white race, the real worth of the backward black.

It is difficult to see how anybody can trace the life and work of the comparatively small band of Negro leaders, during these forty years past, without a profound feeling of admiration for their Christian character, their patience, their wisdom, and their fine sense of Christian delicacy, exhibited under trying conditions. Think of the men upon whom God has placed this most difficult and delicate task of laying the foundation for a totally new relation toward a more numerous and powerful race, and then try to remember how very few have seriously blundered! Think of their task of remaking their relations with a people who were recently their masters! Think of their task of teaching themselves (and in such true way that the members of the other race will also accept the lesson) to live as free black men with white men, on the same soil, and amid the same surroundings, as of yore! Then say whether you can withhold your chivalrous sympathy, or your resolve to help on the learning of the lesson so utterly essential to the peace of both races.

The Negro has had, and still has, this tremendous task laid upon him of making the place which is his in life; and of taking it, not because he demands it, but because he has successfully made that place. In general, he who has to *demand* his place, has never *earned* it. In general, too, he who has *made* a place has deserved it, and, in the long run, it will be accorded him. The Negroes of education, of refinement, of gifts and of culture, are, too generally, held back from the place they have made. This is partly because of ignorance on the part of white people that such Negroes exist, while the only ones they know are the great majority of ignorant farm hands; partly because of the strange anachronism, "social equality," which cuts straight across race integrity, and nowhere exists even within the single bounds of any race.

The negro people are not standing for social equality among themselves, even though some of their extremists, along with the Japanese, are muddying the stream of concord with a cry of "equality of races." No one can doubt but that sane people of every race will continue to stand for that which God made them—white, yellow, brown, red and black—and will try to keep themselves so. In the long run, all will learn to value most the respect that righteous living and service to mankind merit, and to contend least for that which has not been earned. Whatever the future may bring, whether return to Africa in large numbers, or migration to Haiti as some of their leaders contend, or permanence in America, the duty of each day is to help the Negro to help himself in attaining the fullest preparation for the destiny which God's providence has surely in store for him.

So much for political and social relationships, as between the two races. The Negroes have asked the momentous question, "What is our status?"

So too, in matters concerning the Church, they are asking the same question; not, indeed, as involving membership, but as regards organization. The proposal, made in 1874, to create separate Missionary Jurisdictions, resulted in separate Convocations, in a few Dioceses, some fourteen years later. Its renewal, in 1904, in the form of a Memorial, nearly unanimous, from the colored clergy, resulted, in 1918, in the application of the Canon on the Suffragan Episcopate to those Dioceses which should desire to adopt its provisions. The two Bishops elected by Arkansas and North Carolina have been given all the authority and personal initiative possible under the Canon. That it did not, and does not now, satisfy the full desire of the Memorialists is well known. That the conditions obtaining in the South and not now felt to be needful in the North, constitute ground for local adaptation of the Historic Episcopate, is the judgment of the Memorialists.

The reasons for the petition as "the result of many years of patient observation, study and prayer," are clearly set forth, and may be found in the successive Journals of General Convention from 1904 to 1918. Meanwhile, there are no Negro delegates in the House of Deputies, save one from Liberia and no direct voice, from the more than thirty thousand lay members, to represent their interests in the National body. This does not mean that the race is nowhere heard, or its interest never sought. But it does mean that, in national

Conferences and Boards, to which the Negro has sought entrance, the Church is still slow to grant his request.

The picture is not wholly dark. What are the results which, in the midst of confusion and difficulties, the Negro has been able to achieve?

The statistics for the whole race, here given, are taken from the *Negro Year Book* of 1919. In 1866, the Negroes owned 12,000 homes; in 1919, 600,000. Farms owned in 1866, 20,000; in 1919, 50,000. The wealth, for the two contrasted years, is represented as $20,000,000 and $1,110,000,000.

These figures are very eloquent in their announcement. They do not, and cannot, even begin to tell the story of the supreme devotion, the untiring labor, the self-abasement, the sacrifice, the consummate wisdom, of most of that small company of real Negro leaders, who, from the '80s down to now, have accepted the responsibility, and performed the tremendous task, of retrieving the losses of Reconstruction and inspiring the race with an indomitable will to move forward. For this company of leaders was from among the 3.6% of those in professional service, as teachers, doctors, lawyers and the like. Upon them fell the sacred task of guiding the remaining 96.4%, less than 10% of whom were literate. There is no more interesting reading than that which the story of these leaders presents; and that of the trade-schools, farmers' conferences, educational rallies, and religious institutes.

And how was the progress accomplished? It began with the veritable crusade of constructive service preached by the leaders.

"If educated men and women of the race will see and acknowledge the necessity of practical industrial training, and go to work with a zeal and determination, their example will be followed by others who are now without ambition of any kind. The race cannot hope to come into its own until the young colored men and women make up their minds to assist in the general development along these lines. The elder men and women trained in the hard school of slavery, and who so long possessed all the labor—skilled and unskilled—of the South, are dying out; their places must be filled by their children, or we shall lose our hold upon these occupations. Again, Phillips Brooks gave expression to the sentiment: 'One generation gathers the material, and the next builds the palaces.' As I understand it, he wished to inculcate the idea that one generation lays the foundation for succeeding generations."

This is a sample of the messages of these crusaders, borne in varying cadences throughout the race. The appeal was to the cultured, by precept and even more by example, to stimulate the ambition of the whole race; to realize that foundation-building is the task of each generation, and that the neglect of one generation means loss to itself and the next.

But they were not preaching only. They did what they exhorted others to do. With the help of white friends, they began to build schools, and to teach those who could teach others the value of industry and thrift, and the blessings of the self-respect that is unafraid to face life and contribute to its needs. And thus the army of teachers began to go forth. Most of them were not well prepared, and are not at this day, for the calls have been so hurried that the preparation has been equally so.

Today there are 38,000 teachers, against the 600 in 1866; most of them in the little country schools; many under most difficult conditions and impossible surroundings, both of which are rapidly improving under the kindly interest of the dominant whites. And, too, there are many thousands, trained to a degree in the various trades, and taking their places in the industrial life of their homes. The fact that, in 1866, 95% were illiterate, and now only 20%, stands as a living monument to the devoted leaders of these forty years past.

What then is the status of the Negro in American life? Our forefathers fought for liberty to bestow it on all when the time came that the humblest members were prepared to assume its responsibilities. A later generation fought for Democracy—that crowning and pervading principle of liberty. Our great leaders have been as wise, as clear, as simple in the interpretation of democracy as their forefathers were in that of liberty. Shall the Church of God be wise enough, and devoted enough, and fearless enough, to lead the people of God to realize what has been purchased with blood and consecrated by sacrifice?

Now, as then, self-interest engenders prejudice; prejudice of class towards other classes, of crafts towards other crafts, of race towards other races. All the prejudice is not on one side; but no white man, with an eye to justice, can fail to admit the Negro has far the greater cause for his prejudice.

The very existence of different crafts and classes, and still more of different races occupying the same national home, makes problems. The only solution that really solves is Justice, with its accompanying weight in the balance—Mercy. Without the exercise of these, no class or race could hope for continuous life or persistent growth. Where truth and justice meet together, righteousness and peace will kiss each other in a brotherly, harmonious relation, that only the devil's lies and cruel injustice ever mar and distort.

The Negro has been free for sixty years and more. Building upon the wonderfully fine foundation of the past (in spite of manifold and manifest flaws in its making), he has reared racial structures of social, commercial, industrial and religious life, that command respect and admiration. The credit belongs to both races—to the Negro himself, but no less to the race which was once his owner, and whose hand is clearly seen in the building.

The Negro knows even better than his white critics how faulty a living building is in which the majority of the living stones are still rough, unpolished, unsquared. He asks, and he has the right which God gives to His people to ask, that, as a free man, he be treated as a man; that, as justice is the right of life, he be accorded it; that, as a citizen, he be granted the rights of citizenship—the equal right of life, liberty and the pursuit of happiness; that laws governing citizenship be applied with equal justice to Negroes and to Whites.

If the Church of God (that is, her members) can bring herself to stand for less than that, it is difficult to find ground for forgiveness at the hands of the Son of Man who died upon the Cross for the salvation of all.

Of course there is a problem; but the real problem is not how to escape doing justice, but how to be just without destroying racial integrity. Race and family are of God's institution, God's alone, and their respective relations are of His making. Both are written in God's handwriting, in flesh and blood; not in man's, on scraps of paper. But this phase of the subject is exceedingly large. The apology for its introduction here, is to be found in the emphasis which it seeks to lay upon the ultimate purpose of education and training.

When one considers the few years from Emancipation, the reflection must come that long, long steps forward have been taken; and who can doubt that where unalloyed interest in the progress of the black members reigns in the hearts of the white, the guidance of the loving Father has stayed our impatience? Who can doubt that, in His guiding providence, He will deal with us according to His lovingkindness?

APPENDIX

NOTE 1

(CHAPTER VI, PAGE 159)

THE HOSPITAL WAS THE RESULT OF THE DEVOTED WORK OF THE REV. DR. AND MRS. HUNTER, THE LATTER MAKING THIS HER SPECIAL CHARGE, RAISING MOST OF THE FUNDS, AND KEEPING THEM SEPARATE FROM THOSE OF THE SCHOOL.

THE EARLIER PRINCIPALS OF THE SCHOOL ITSELF EACH PERFORMED DISTINCTIVE SERVICES WHICH WON THE AFFECTION AND GRATITUDE OF THE CHURCH IN NORTH CAROLINA. THE REV. DR. J. BRINTON SMITH FOUNDED THE SCHOOL IN HIS FIVE YEARS OF SERVICE FROM 1867 TO 1872. THE REV. DR. JOHN E. C. SMEDE NOURISHED IT THROUGH THE MOST DIFFICULT RECONSTRUCTION PERIOD, 1872 TO 1884, WHEN TENSION WAS HIGH, AND WHEN SYMPATHY BETWEEN NORTH AND SOUTH AND WHITE AND BLACK WAS AT ITS LOWEST EBB. THE REV. DR. ROBERT B. SUTTON, 1884-1891, SUCCEEDED TO AN ATMOSPHERE OF RELAXED WEARINESS FOLLOWING THE LONG DRAWN-OUT CONTROVERSIES OVER THE "RACE QUESTION," WHEN SUPPORT WAS MOST DIFFICULT, THE MORE SO BECAUSE THE CHURCH HAD NO SETTLED POLICY OF SCHOOL WORK FOR THE NEGROES. EACH HAD A TASK REQUIRING ALL HIS FINE ABILITY.

IT IS NO REFLECTION ON OTHERS (FOR COMPARISON IS IMPOSSIBLE WHERE THE TIMES AND TASKS WERE SO DISTINCT) TO SAY THAT THE REV. DR. HUNTER'S GREAT CONTRIBUTION WAS THE COMPLETE REORGANIZATION OF THE EDUCATIONAL IDEAL OF ST. AUGUSTINE'S, AND ITS REFOUNDING ON THE DEVOTED AND HEROIC LABORS OF HIS PREDECESSORS. DR. HUNTER'S 25 YEARS OF SERVICE CONTRIBUTED MOST POWERFULLY TO THE MOVEMENT WHICH MADE THE CHURCH INSTITUTE POSSIBLE, AS WELL AS TO THE PRESENT STRONG GROWTH TOWARD A SOLID FOUNDATION FOR THE CHRISTIAN EDUCATION OF THE NEGROES. HE BECAME DR. SUTTON'S ASSISTANT, WHEN THE "MODERN PERIOD" BEGAN. OLD THINGS WERE PASSING AWAY, AND THE NEW HAD YET TO BE FASHIONED. THE MODERN EDUCATIONAL SYSTEM WAS JUST BEGINNING TO BE REALIZED IN THE SOUTH. DR. HUNTER BROUGHT YOUTH, VIGOR AND ABILITY TO THE TASK NOT ONLY OF JUSTIFYING THE WISDOM OF THE FATHERS BUT OF FULFILLING THE OFFICE OF THE WISE STEWARD IN BRINGING FORTH OLD AND NEW TREASURES TO ENRICH

THE PRESENT AND THE FUTURE. HE WAS ABLY SECONDED BY MRS. HUNTER, AND BY HIS ASSISTANT WHO IS NOW BISHOP DELANY.

THE REV. EDGAR H. GOOLD, FOR FOUR YEARS DR. HUNTER'S ASSISTANT, IS NOW THE PRINCIPAL. HE IS A GRADUATE OF AMHERST COLLEGE AND OF THE GENERAL THEOLOGICAL SEMINARY.

NOTE 2
(CHAPTER VI, PAGE 159)

JAMES SOLOMON RUSSELL WAS BORN OF SLAVE PARENTS IN MECKLENBURG, VA., DEC. 20TH, 1827. THE NAME SOLOMON WAS BESTOWED BY HIS MOTHER WITH THE PRAYER THAT THE LITTLE ONE WOULD INHERIT THE WISDOM OF HIS NAMESAKE; AND THE PRAYER HAS BEEN ANSWERED, FOR THIS BOY HAS RIPENED INTO ONE OF THE WISEST OF HIS PEOPLE. A WAR-BOY, HIS EARLY YEARS WERE SUBJECTED TO THE PRIVATIONS OF THE GENERAL POVERTY OF THE TIMES. AT TWELVE YEARS HIS SCHOOLING BEGAN, THE BOY PAYING HIS WAY PARTLY BY SELLING BUTTER AND EGGS, AND, FOR THE BALANCE, HIS LABOR. HAMPTON WAS THE EARTHLY GOAL OF THE YOUNG COLORED YOUTHS OF THAT TIME, AND RUSSELL ATTAINED IT. FROM HAMPTON HE ENTERED MAJOR COOKE'S SCHOOL IN PETERSBURG, AND GRADUATED FROM THE THEOLOGICAL DEPARTMENT, IN 1882. UPON BEING ORDERED A DEACON, HE WAS AT ONCE APPOINTED MISSIONARY TO BRUNSWICK AND MECKLENBURG COUNTIES, WITH RESIDENCE AT LAWRENCEVILLE. WITHIN EIGHT MONTHS HE BROUGHT HIS WIFE, MISS VIRGINIA M. MORGAN, TO MAKE THE HAPPY HOME WHICH HAS BEEN THE HAVEN OF THE BUSIEST MAN OF HIS RACE IN THE WORLD, WITH THE EXCEPTION OF DR. WASHINGTON. MRS. RUSSELL, UNTIL HER DEATH TWO YEARS AGO, WAS AS VITAL TO THE LIFE OF THE SCHOOL AS WAS HER HUSBAND. IN 1917, THE VIRGINIA SEMINARY CONFERRED THE DEGREE OF DOCTOR OF DIVINITY ON MR. RUSSELL, THE FIRST PERSON OF COLOR TO RECEIVE THIS HONOR SO RARELY BESTOWED UPON ANYONE BY THAT VENERABLE SEMINARY. ONCE HAS DR. RUSSELL DECLINED ELECTION TO THE EPISCOPATE, AND ONCE AGAIN TO HAVE HIS NAME PRESENTED. HE FELT THE URGE OF DUTY TOO STRONGLY AT LAWRENCEVILLE TO ALLOW HIMSELF TO BE DIVERTED. FOR MANY YEARS HE HAS BEEN ARCHDEACON OF SOUTHERN VIRGINIA, AND THE MOST CONSPICUOUSLY WISE LEADER AMONG THE 400,000 NEGROES OF THE DIOCESE.

AS A DEACON, HE OPENED A SCHOOL IN THE VESTRY-ROOM OF THE LITTLE CHURCH BUILT BY HIS OWN EFFORTS. MRS. RUSSELL AND HIMSELF WERE THE TEACHERS. THE POPULATION WAS 88 PER CENT ILLITERATE, and correspondingly prejudiced and superstitious. The story of the transformation is a romance of absorbing interest. The teacher was a travelling missionary, without other means than nature had provided for transporting himself over great distances. He pleaded for a horse before the Diocesan Convention. "Let's give Brother Russell a horse," was the response, and "Ida" became as well known as Russell himself over two large "black-belt" counties. So Russell and Ida became the missionary team, each producing fruit after its kind. The Archdeacon's pupils became scouts and recruits in the forward army against sin and ignorance; Ida's colts increased the transportation facilities of workers.

In the midst of besetting difficulties, the young priest found a steady sympathetic helper in Mrs. Buford whose daughter became the wife of the late Bishop of East Carolina. She had started a hospital for infirm colored people, and now extended her interest to the school.

NOTE 4
(Chapter VII, page 180)

The Methodist Bishop, William Capers, father of the late Bishop of South Carolina and grandfather of the Bishop of West Texas, gave much of his life to the Negro. No better witness can be found of the power of Jesus Christ over the life of those Negroes whom He specially called. These samples from Bishop Capers' Autobiography are selected, his description regretfully abridged:

"The most remarkable man in Fayetteville (N. C.) when I went there, and who died during my stay, was a Negro by the name of Henry Evans. I say the most remarkable in view of his class; and I call him Negro with unfeigned respect. The name simply designates the race, and it is vulgar to regard it with opprobrium. I have known and loved and honored not a few Negroes in my lifetime, who were probably as pure of heart as Evans, or anybody else. Such were my old friends, Castile Selby and John Boquet, of Charleston; Will Campbell and Harry Myrick, of Wilmington; York Cohen, of Savannah; and others I might name. These I might call remarkable for their goodness. But I use the word in a broader sense for Henry Evans, who was confessedly the father of the Methodist Church, black and white, in Fayetteville, and the best preacher of his time in that quarter; and who was so remarkable, as to have become the greatest curiosity of the town; insomuch that distinguished visitors hardly felt that they might pass a Sunday in Fayetteville without hearing him preach."

Henry Evans was a shoemaker in Virginia, licensed to preach by the Methodists. Being free, he decided to move to Charleston. On the way, Fayetteville detained him. His spirit was stirred at perceiving the ungodliness of his people. There was no religion of any denomination, so Evans began preaching to his people. The Town Council objected, and he withdrew to the sandhills nearby. The results upon the changing lives were notable. Evans explained his motives to the authorities; and this, with the fruits of his work, won the day; he was allowed the liberty of the town. Mistresses and masters, powerfully influenced by the great improvement in their servants, began to attend the services. They built a frame structure for the preaching, with seats for the Whites and a projection for Evans' home. It became too small and was enlarged, for the Whites now occupied all of the original building, the Negroes the addition. "That," continues Bishop Capers, "was the identical state of the case when I was pastor. Often was I in that shed, and much to my edification. I have known not many preachers who appeared more conversant with Scripture than Evans, and whose conversation was more instructive as to the things of God. He seemed always deeply impressed with the responsibility of his position; and not even our old friend Castile was more remarkable for his humble and deferential deportment towards the Whites than Evans was. Nor would he allow any partiality of his friends to induce him to vary, in the least degree, the line of conduct or the bearing which he had prescribed for himself in this respect; never speaking to a white man but with his hat under his arm, never allowing himself to be seated in their houses; and even confining himself to the kind and manner of dress proper for Negroes in general, except his plain black coat for the pulpit. 'The Whites are kind to me, and come to hear me preach; but I belong to my own sort, and must not spoil them.' And yet, Henry Evans was a Boanerges; and, in his duty, feared not the face of man."

He died, Mr. Capers ministering to him, in 1810, his last breath drawn in the act of pronouncing, "Thanks be to God which giveth us the victory through our Lord Jesus Christ."

BISHOP CAPERS CONTINUES: "ON THE SUNDAY BEFORE EVANS' DEATH, DURING THIS MEETING, THE LITTLE DOOR BETWEEN HIS HUMBLE SHED AND THE CHANCEL WHERE I STOOD, WAS OPEN; AND THE DYING MAN ENTERED FOR A LAST FAREWELL TO HIS PEOPLE. HE WAS ALMOST TOO FEEBLE TO STAND AT ALL, BUT SUPPORTING HIMSELF BY THE RAILING OF THE CHANCEL HE SAID, 'I HAVE COME TO SAY MY LAST WORD TO YOU. IT IS THIS: NONE BUT CHRIST. THREE TIMES I HAVE HAD MY LIFE IN JEOPARDY FOR PREACHING THE GOSPEL TO YOU. THREE TIMES I HAVE BROKEN THE ICE ON THE EDGE OF THE WATER AND SWUM ACROSS THE CAPE FEAR TO PREACH THE GOSPEL TO YOU. AND NOW, IF IN MY LAST HOUR, I COULD TRUST TO THAT, OR TO ANYTHING ELSE BUT TO CHRIST CRUCIFIED FOR MY SALVATION, ALL WOULD BE LOST, AND MY SOUL PERISH FOREVER.' A NOBLE TESTIMONY, WORTHY, NOT OF EVANS ONLY, BUT OF SAINT PAUL! HIS FUNERAL AT THE CHURCH WAS ATTENDED BY A GREATER CONCOURSE OF PERSONS THAN HAD BEEN SEEN ON ANY FUNERAL OCCASION BEFORE. THE WHOLE COMMUNITY APPEARED TO MOURN HIS DEATH, AND THE UNIVERSAL FEELING SEEMED TO BE THAT, IN HONORING THE MEMORY OF HENRY EVANS, WE WERE PAYING A TRIBUTE TO VIRTUE AND RELIGION. HE WAS BURIED UNDER THE CHANCEL OF THE CHURCH OF WHICH HE HAD BEEN IN SO REMARKABLE A MANNER THE FOUNDER."

HENRY EVANS WAS OF THE LITERATE CLASS; NOT EDUCATED IN THE SENSE OF THIS DAY, BUT OF HIS DAY, WHEN THE BIBLE WAS FAR MORE THE BOOK OF CHRISTIAN PEOPLE THAN IT IS NOW; AND HENRY EVANS, WAS "WISER THAN HIS TEACHERS."

NOTE 5

(CHAPTER VII, PAGE 185)

ATTENTION MAY BE CALLED TO TWO NOTABLE NEGRO LEADERS OF THE EARLY NINETEENTH CENTURY.

THE REV. WILLIAM DOUGLASS, THE SON OF A BLACKSMITH, BORN IN BALTIMORE IN 1805, MADE HIS WAY INTO THE METHODIST MINISTRY. WHILE AT WORK ON THE EASTERN SHORE, HE SOUGHT EPISCOPAL ORDERS, AND WAS ORDAINED BY BISHOP STONE IN ST. STEPHEN'S, CECIL COUNTY. "IN THE EVENING," WROTE THE BISHOP, "THE CHURCH WAS GIVEN UP TO THE COLORED PEOPLE, AND THE REV. MR. DOUGLASS preached to them an interesting sermon." This was on June 22, 1834. The same year he was called to St. Thomas' African Church, Philadelphia, which, since the death, in 1818, of its founder, the Rev. Absalom Jones, had been served by one and another of the white rectors of the city. On February 14, 1836, Mr. Douglass was advanced to the priesthood. Bishop Onderdonk who officiated, wrote, "Mr. Douglass is a man of color. I take the opportunity of recording my very high estimate of his highly respectable intellect and most amiable qualities which entirely relieved my mind, in his case, from the anxieties that I had long felt in regard to this department of Episcopal duty. He ministers to a congregation entirely at unity in itself, much attached to him, and improving under his pastoral care in principles and duties of our common Christianity."

Mr. Douglass became a leader of power among his race. Bishop Alonzo Potter, in announcing his death to the Convention of 1862, said, "It hath pleased the Lord to call away from the Church Militant the Rev. William Douglass, rector of St. Thomas' African Church, in this city, where he has ministered for the last twenty-seven years—a man of great modesty, of ripe scholarship, and of much more than ordinary talents and prudence. He is, as far as I am informed, the only clergyman of unmixed African descent, who, in this country, has published work of considerable magnitude. In two volumes, one of sermons and one a history of St. Thomas' Church, he has vindicated his right to appear among our respected divines. As a reader of the Liturgy he was unsurpassed."

The Rev. Alexander Crummell, D.D., was born in New York in 1819. He was early baptized by the Rev. Peter Williams of St. Philip's Church, under whom he was trained in the Church's ways. In early manhood he applied for Orders. The General Theological Seminary declined to admit Negroes as students at that time, and Crummell was prepared for ordination in Boston. In 1842, he was ordained by Bishop Griswold. Dr. Clark, later Bishop of Rhode Island, was one of the examiners, and years afterwards the impression then strongly made was thus recorded: "I was appointed, with the late Rev. Dr. William Croswell, to examine young Crummell when he applied for deacon's orders in the Diocese of Massachusetts; and I remember that Dr. Croswell afterwards remarked to me that no candidate for the ministry had ever passed through his hands who had given him more entire satisfaction." After a brief year in Providence, R. I., Mr. Crummell answered the earnest call then coming from Liberia, and threw in his life with his colored brethren there. He was at once missionary, teacher, and the trainer of the theological students. Once he left Liberia for a stay in England, and returned with a Cambridge degree. After the Civil War, he returned to America, and, in Washington, founded St. Luke's Church, whose corner-stone Bishop Pinckney laid in 1876. For more than twenty years he was its rector.

No man of the race in his day was more worthily esteemed, or more worthy of it, than Alexander Crummell, and none more truly an apostle of his Lord.

NOTE 6

(CHAPTER VII, PAGE *185*)

The Colony of Georgia affords another interesting illustration. It was the result of James Oglethorpe's venture in colonizing debtor-prisoners and other unfortunates, a movement characterized as "the beginning of modern philanthropy," and giving an opportunity to those noted missionaries of the Church of England, John and Charles Wesley and George Whitfield. Slavery was to be forbidden in the colony; but circumstances proved too strong. Rice was the staple crop, the waters formed its congenial home, and the Negroes—who else could so well subdue the swamps and make them productive? The result was inevitable. Georgia conformed to the general policy of her sister colonies.

As philanthropy was the motive, so religion was the animating spirit, of the new colony. Accordingly John and Charles Wesley were among the first colonists. The former established Christ Church Parish, Savannah, which was later divided, allowing the formation of Christ Church Parish, Frederica, named for the Savannah mother-church, Charles Wesley being its first rector, in 1736. These were deadly pioneer days, and rectors came thick and fast as predecessors were driven out, sometimes by political influence, most often by climatic.

Charles Wesley remained a year, and then John, his brother, assumed the charge of both parishes, making his way to

Frederica on foot, trusting, for the crossing of the large rivers, to the passing canoes of the friendly Indians. "The fact of these visits to Frederica has been questioned," writes the Rev. D. W. Winn, the present rector, "but the writer has seen Wesley's own diary in which he tells how he fell into the water from a small boat while embarking from Frederica, and the leaves of the diary showed the marks of the water." Mr. Winn, the descendant of the sister of those first missionaries, Charles and John Wesley, and fourteenth rector in succession from them, has had more than ordinary interest in the labors of his predecessors and in the knowledge of them. George Whitfield succeeded the Wesleys in 1737 or '38; and, after them, three other missionaries of the period of establishment. The last, the Rev. Bartholomew Zorabuhler, was also the first of the line of permanent workers, serving from 1746 to 1766. Frederica, the chief centre of Negro missions, furnishes our sample for the study of this early work in Georgia. The English Church Commissary, succeeding Commissary Bray for a part of the period, was the Rev. J. Ottolonghe, who made his headquarters in Savannah, and directed the Church's enterprises in the colony.

Happily we have access to some of the early reports of the Commissary describing the Negro work, these being kindly furnished by the Rev. James Lawrence, present historiographer of the Diocese. These are written with punctilious regard to the picturesquely bad spelling of the days of "Bloody Mary" and "Good Queen Bess," one line only, in original, is here inflicted; it is dated Dec. 5, 1751. "In my last sent you by ye *Charming Martha* I took ye liberty to acquaint you with my safe arrival in Georgia." The lonely Commissary takes large liberty in thus addressing his home-superiors through the intermediary, not of a charming spinster, but of a boat whose picture would belie the description; and he notes, in appropriate capitals, his arrival, safe from peril, to which a good 20 per cent of the adventurers of the time fell victims.

The letter proceeds: "As soon as the Fatigue of the Voyage permitted it, I desired Reverend Zouberbuyler (Zorabuhler, Mr. Winn says; but what matters such a liberty with names among friends?) that he would be so good as to give the people notice in the Church that I would instruct their Negroes three days in the week, viz.: Sundays, Tuesdays and Thursdays, which he accordingly did, and that I might make it easier to the Masters of these unhappy Creatures, I have appointed the Time of their coming to me to be at Night, when their daily Labour is done. When we meet, I make them go to Prayers with me, having composed for the purpose a few Prayers, suitable (I hope) to the Occasion. Having thus recommended Ourselves to the Protection of Heaven, and for his Blessing on our Undertaking; I instruct them to Reade, that they may be able in Time to comfort themselves in reading the Book of God. After this is done, I make them repeat the Lord's Prayer and the Belief, and a Short Portion of the Catechism, explaining to them in as easie and Familiar a manner as I can the Meaning of what they repeat, and before I part with them, I make a Discourse to them on the Being of God, or the Life and Death of our adorable Redeemer, or upon some of ye Precepts of the Holy Gospel, generally introducing some Event or Story, taken out of the Bible, suitable to the Discourse in Hand; and in order to get their Love, I use them with all the Kindness and endearing Words that I am capable of, which makes them willing to come to me and ready to follow my Advice, and as Rewards are Springs that set less selfish Minds than these unhappy Creatures possess, on Motion, I have therefore promised to reward the Industrious and Diligent, and Hope through Christ's Grace, that 'twill have its due Effect. These then, Dear Sir, are the Methods, these the Path, that I have chalked out in order to discharge my Duty. If right and agreeable to your better Judgement, I shall continue in them; if not, I shall be very ready to put in Practice any other Method, which you shall please to prescribe."

As the efforts expand and the field is enlarged, new difficulties are met. In 1754, the Commissary has pushed out among the new arrivals. A more stable government had encouraged the expansion of planting interests. There were great difficulties to be met in reaching the Negroes of the new expansions. "Our Negroes," he writes, referring to the new plantations, "are so ignorant of the English language, and none can be found to talk in their own, that it is a great while before you can get them to understand what the meaning of Words is. Again Slavery is certainly a great Depresser of the Mind, which retards their learning a new Religion proposed to them in a new and unknown Language, besides the Superstitions of a false Religion to be combatted with, and nothing harder to be removed (you know) than prejudices of education, riveted by Time and intrenched in deep Ignorance." So there was anguish of heart all along the line.

In 1858, the Commissary's letter clearly infers another peril to his efforts growing out of the quarrels of Christian denominations. A Church-Bill was presented to the Assembly seeking to better the conditions of the Slaves in all ways possible. But the Assembly was composed of a large majority of Dissenters, and the bill was presented by Church of England representatives—fair ground apparently for religious disputes which lost sight of bill, of Negroes, of religion and of justice.

It was the age of materialism which, as Professor Brawley says, "defeated the benevolence of Oglethorpe's scheme for the founding of Georgia," and against which the Church battled, not only on behalf of the slaves, but for the very life of religion. A difficult battle it was when self-interest was all arrayed on the side of materialism.

In his evident great zeal and anxiety, the Commissary was warmly followed by the Rev. Mr. Zorabuhler of Frederica, under whom that parish was fixed to include the "Town of Frederica, with the islands of Great and Little St. Simon's, and the adjacent islands," and the name changed to St. James'.

Throughout the Revolutionary period, the Missions were probably served from Savannah. Recovery from the disasters of war was very slow, and it was not until after the consecration of Bishop Elliott, in 1841, that the Church became organized for work. Only three clergymen were in Georgia to organize the primary Convention of the Diocese, in 1823.

In his first address to this Convention, Bishop Elliott said: "The religious instruction of our domestics, and of the Negroes upon plantations, is a subject that never should be passed over in the address of a Southern Bishop." Six years later, he enlarged upon what he deemed to be a worthy ministry to them. He spoke from experience.

"During the last week, I visited the Mission upon the North side of the Ogeeche River, under the charge of the Rev. William C. Williams. A neat country church has been erected by some of the planters of that side of the river, which was sufficiently completed for service but not for consecration. I officiated in it on Sunday, the 18th of April, when eight candidates were presented for Confirmation, the first fruits of the earnest labor of their missionary. Mr. Williams is pursuing the only plan that will be of any service with this class of our population, identifying himself with their spiritual condition, and going in and out among them as their pastor and guide. It is my earnest hope that our Episcopal planters will take this matter into consideration, and make arrangements for the employment of missionaries of their own Church, so that Masters and Servants may worship together in unity of spirit and in the bond of peace. It would tend very much to strengthen the relation of Masters and Servants, by bringing into action the highest and holiest feelings of our common nature. There should be much less danger of inhumanity on the one side, and of insubordination on the other, between parties who knelt upon the Lord's day around the same Table and were partakers of the same Communion."

The Ogeeche Mission has an interesting history of continuous life from 1847 to the present day. It is ten miles from Savannah in the heart of the then great rice fields, where two Churches—St. Mark's the first, and still used, and St. Barnabas', now decayed—were built. The Negroes were utterly illiterate, and remained so until about 1890, when Mr. Dodge built a school, and the younger ones were taught. The services were committed to memory by that very large congregation, and the responses were, and are, "as the sound of many waters"; the singing, like a great organ. No instrument was used. The "Clark" for about fifty years was a very big, commanding, black member with magnificent voice, who, at the proper time for chant or hymn, stood before the congregation, sounded the note, raised the tune, and both led and inspired the singers. The habit still continues.

The Rev. Mr. Winn, for a long time their rector, wrote this tribute in November, 1921. "They knew the Service and took part in a way to make one's heart glow, and which would put any white city congregation to shame. To minister to and among them was an inspiration, even though physical

CONDITIONS AS TO LOCOMOTION, ETC., WERE TRYING. I HAVE DEALT WITH NEGROES FROM THE TIME OF MY 'BLACK MAMMY' MOLINDA, WHO WAS 'NO COMMON NIGGER' BUT A 'MOLLY GLOSSY NIGGER,' HAVING COME FROM MADAGASCAR; BUT WHILE I COULD UNDERSTAND ANYTHING SAID TO ME WHILE LOOKING THE SPEAKER IN THE FACE AND PAYING CLOSE ATTENTION, YET, WHEN ONE OF THEM SPOKE TO ANOTHER, IT WAS MOSTLY AN UNKNOWN TONGUE TO ME.

"BISHOP NELSON, LATE OF GEORGIA, SAID THAT A SERVICE AMONG THOSE RICE-FIELD NEGROES WAS THE MOST SPLENDID THING HE EVER EXPERIENCED. THAT WAS MY EXPERIENCE ALSO; FOR, EXCEPTING THE GREAT PROCESSION AND SERVICE AT THE LAYING OF THE CORNERSTONE OF THE WASHINGTON CATHEDRAL, SOME EIGHTEEN YEARS AGO, THERE HAS NOT BEEN, IN MY 41 YEARS OF MINISTRY, ANY APPROACH TO THE JOY OF A SERVICE AMONG THOSE NEGROES. IT WAS NOT MERELY ENTHUSIASM—I COULD AROUSE THAT AMONG ANY CONGREGATION OF NEGROES—IT WAS APPREHENSION, APPRECIATION, AND THE OUTPOURING OF THE SOUL."

THERE IS PERHAPS NO CONGREGATION IN THE SOUTH UPON WHICH THE RAVAGES OF WAR HAD SO LITTLE EFFECT. LATER CHANGES HAVE GREATLY REDUCED THEIR NUMBER, BUT THE OLD HABITS REMAIN. THE OFFERING IS STILL, IN PART, EGGS OR OTHER FARM PRODUCE AS REVERENTLY OFFERED AS THE MONEY AND COINS IN THE SILVER ALMSBASINS OF THE CITY-CHURCH.

THE REPORTS OF GEORGIA PARISHES IN 1860, SHOW THAT PRACTICALLY ALL WERE MINISTERING TO THE NEGROES. IN ADDITION TO THE EXTENDED WORK OF FREDERICA PARISH AND ST. MARK'S, OGEECHE, ST. STEPHEN'S CHAPEL, SAVANNAH, HAD BEEN ESTABLISHED IN '56, ESPECIALLY FOR THE NEGROES, AND WAS THE BASE OF MISSION-WORK ON NEARBY PLANTATIONS.

NOTE 7

(CHAPTER VII, PAGE 185)

REGARDING THE INSTRUCTION IN RELIGION GIVEN TO THE NEGROES BY THEIR WHITE OWNERS, THE FOLLOWING MAY BE OF INTEREST.

IT IS ONLY OCCASIONALLY THAT ONE FINDS A RECORD LIKE THIS: "IN 1712 THE REV. GILBERT JONES WAS RECTOR OF CHRIST CHURCH PARISH. HE FELT A GREAT INTEREST IN THE SPIRITUAL WELFARE OF THE NEGROES, AND ENDEAVORED TO PERSUADE THEIR OWNERS TO ASSIST IN HAVING THEM INSTRUCTED IN THE CHRISTIAN FAITH; BUT HE FOUND THIS GOOD WORK LAY UNDER DIFFICULTIES AS YET INSUPERABLE."

Generally the testimony is most favorable and encouraging, as, for example, "The Rev. William Taylor wrote to the Society in 1713, stating that Mrs. Haig and Mrs. Edwards, who lately came to the plantations in Carolina, have taken extraordinary pains to instruct a considerable number of Negroes in the principles of the Christian religion, and to reclaim and reform them. The wonderful success they met with in about six months, encouraged me to go and examine the Negroes about their knowledge in Christianity. They declared to me their faith in the chief articles of our religion, which they sufficiently explained. They rehearsed by heart, very distinctly, the Creed, the Lord's Prayer, and the Ten Commandments. Fourteen of them gave me so great satisfaction, and were so desirous to be baptized, that I thought it my duty to do it on the last Lord's Day. I doubt not but these gentlewomen will prepare the rest of them for Baptism in a little time, and I hope their good example will provoke some masters and mistresses to take the same care and pains with their poor Negroes."

NOTE 8

(Chapter VII, Page 186)

About 1834, an unknown writer, in South Carolina (a journal published by the State Agricultural Department) makes this significant statement which is strong testimony to the advancement of the race: "Despite the injunction, 'Judge not,' it has been asserted that the morality of the Negroes is not in proportion to their religious fervor. A class, marked as distinctly by their inferior social position as they are by race, invites such charges which are far more sweeping than just. If morality be the fruit of religion, it is not surprising (wonderful as the progress of the African in South Carolina has been) that morality has not, in one century and a half, attained the maturity, among the colored race, which has been the result of nearly nineteen centuries of Christian teachings to the European. Nevertheless, it would be a great mistake to suppose that any people exhibit in a higher degree that instinctive faith in the existence of absolute justice, truth, and goodness, which marks the capacity of human nature alike for religion and for morality, than do the colored people of this State."

NOTE 9

(CHAPTER VII, PAGE 186)

"RESOLVED, 1, THAT IT IS UNNECESSARY AT PRESENT FOR THIS BODY TO TAKE MEASURES FOR THE FORMATION OF ANY FUND FOR SUPPORTING MISSIONARIES TO THE COLORED PEOPLE; IT BEING UNDERSTOOD THAT THE DIFFICULTY IS RATHER TO OBTAIN THE MISSIONARIES, THAN THE MEANS OF SUPPORTING THEM.

"... 5. THAT THIS CONVENTION HAVE HEARD, WITH GREAT SATISFACTION, OF THE EMPLOYMENT, BY PROPRIETORS OF ESTATES ON THE WATEREE AND IN PRINCE WILLIAMS PARISH, OF MISSIONARIES OF OUR CHURCH, FOR THE RELIGIOUS INSTRUCTION OF THEIR COLORED PEOPLE."

AND THE REASON IS SIGNIFICANTLY, THOUGH PERHAPS UNCONSCIOUSLY, GIVEN IN THESE TWO EXTRACTS FROM THE SAME ISSUE:

"WATEREE MISSION—94 COLORED COMMUNICANTS. A DECIDED RELIGIOUS INFLUENCE PREVAILS AMONG THE NEGROES, FOR MANY ARE ACTING ON PRINCIPLES BUT RECENTLY KNOWN TO THEM. SUNDAY SERVICES ON PLANTATION, 45 TIMES."

NOTE 10

(CHAPTER VII, PAGE 189)

FROM THE MANY WHO WROUGHT DEVOTEDLY AND MIGHTILY AND LOVINGLY AMONG THE PLANTATION NEGROES, THERE STAND OUT A FEW MEN WHOM THEIR CONTEMPORARIES WOULD HAVE SINGLED OUT FOR PECULIAR HONORS. AND IT SURELY IS A PECULIAR HONOR TO MERIT NOTE AMONG THE ABLE SPIRITS WHO FORMED THE STAFF OF MISSIONARIES; FOR THE CHURCH ENTRUSTED THE SPIRITUAL CARE OF THE NEGRO TO HER ABLEST AND BEST. AMONG THEM ALL, THE REV. ALEXANDER GLENNIE, RECTOR OF ALL SAINTS, WACCAMAW, 1832-1866, MUST HOLD A PLACE ALL HIS OWN IN THE ANNALS OF TIME. FOR THIRTY-FOUR YEARS HE WAS THE SHEPHERD OF THE NEGRO FOLDS OF THE WACCAMAW AREA. DURING THOSE YEARS THE NEEDS OF HIS FLOCK; THE WISE WAY TO PROVIDE THEM; THEIR CAPACITY, INTELLECTUAL AND SPIRITUAL; THE FOOD NEEDFUL FOR SOUL SUSTENANCE; THE SOCIAL CRAVINGS, AND HOW TO PROVIDE WHOLESOME GRATIFICATIONS—ALL THESE, AND MORE, WERE MR. GLENNIE'S LIFE STUDY, AND THAT OF HIS LIFE-LONG FRIEND AND CO-WORKER, MR. PLOWDEN WESTON, OF HAGLEY PLANTATION, THE SEAT OF THE LARGEST SINGLE MISSION IN THE FIELD.

Gaining completely and very early the confidence of planters and servants, Mr. Glennie labored in a vast field, restricted only by his powers of endurance, which were enormous. As plantations, one after another, came under his care, chapels were built and filled with well-instructed members and catechumens. By about 1845, in addition to teachers and catechists in large numbers, an Assistant Minister was employed, and, two years later, two. His sermons to the Negroes, published with an introduction by himself, are marvels of beautiful simplicity, the high art of the perfect teacher. In reading his Good Friday sermon, the wonder is how so great and so marvelous a mystery could be so truly and beautifully unfolded in a wealth of one and two-syllable words. And the blessed story loses absolutely nothing from the simplicity of the telling.

In him were combined the art of the teacher and the tending care of the shepherd. "My habit is," he writes, "after concluding the Service, to question the people assembled upon the sermon they have just heard, which enables me to dwell more at large upon matters briefly touched upon in the sermon. This practice, and the frequent use of our Church Catechism, is, I need scarcely say, the most important part of the duty of those engaged in the instruction of Negroes." We might add, in the better instruction of anybody.

NOTE 11
(Chapter VII, page *191*)

Similar to the work of Mr. Glennie and of Mr. Weston (after whom Weston Chapel was named) was that of Mr. Drayton.

The Rev. J. G. Drayton was both a clergyman and a planter, his plantation being the far-famed "Magnolia" in St. Andrew's Parish, of which he was rector. Besides Magnolia chapel built by him, he ministered regularly for many years from about 1850, to two other chapels for the Negroes—Barker's and Magwood's, in the same parish. From a letter of a descendant of Mr. Drayton's, these extracts are quoted rather freely:

"In looking back to them, I now realize how out of the ordinary these Services were; how beautiful the feeling existing between the priest and his people; how simple, sweet, and uplifting it all was—even to a little child—to sit there listening to his words, feeling that greater love through his love. The picture of him that I carry in my memory I wish that I might send to you. One cannot put an influence into words. His face during the prayers; the high, weird singing of the Negroes in the familiar hymns; the breath of the fresh spring woods as it brought the Easter message through the wide windows—all blend to make the memory. I remember, too, a ceremony that was always amusing. It was his habit before service to distribute among the poorest of the congregation a contribution which, later, they placed, with the air of millionaires, in the alms basin. And then, after 'Marse John' had exhorted them to his and their satisfaction, there was a great crowding around his small phaeton. The drive home was frequently made lively, and precarious as well, because of the gifts of 'frizzle fowls' and 'yard aigs.' The roads were often bad and the eggs good, and one had to be careful."

After the destruction of Sherman's raid, being left very poor and the phæton destroyed, Mr. Drayton, though an old man, never faltered but used to walk some twelve or sixteen miles each Sunday to hold at least three services in the houses of the parish. (The chapels were burned in the raid.)

NOTE 12

(Chapter VII, page *197*)

Notable among the founders of schools and parishes was John W. Perry, who spent his life in Tarboro, N. C., as rector, founder of a parochial school, and missionary over a wide area. From his school went his gifted son, now Principal of St. Athanasius', Brunswick, Ga. Another is the Rev. James S. Russell, D. D., founder of St. Paul's School and many missions, and Archdeacon of Southern Virginia. Had it not been for St. Augustine's, and St. Paul's, the Church would be barren indeed of workers. Still another is the Rev. Hutchins C. Bishop, whose strong personality has quickened the life of the Negro churches of New York, and helped to treble their growth. Others are the Rev. Henry S. McDuffy, long a worker in North Carolina, now a fine spiritual power, with Dr. Henry Phillips, in the life of Philadelphia; the Rev. Primus B. Alston, founder of the parish and school in Charlotte, N. C., the soldier of steadfast faith and loyalty; the Rev. Geo. F. Bragg, a church-builder in his first years in Virginia, and for thirty years rector of old St. James', Baltimore, whose intense love for the Church has been contagious, and whose loyalty to his race has been an inspiration to them; the Rev. Geo. G. Middleton, who built his church and rectory in Natchez, Miss., for he was a carpenter and followed his Master in trade and calling; the Rev. William V. Tunnell, Warden and Professor in King Hall and Rector of St. Phillips, Washington, an inspiring teacher in classroom and parish; the Rt. Rev. Henry B. Delaney, D. D., Dean of St. Augustine's Raleigh, his Alma Mater, Archdeacon of Negro Work, and, since 1918, Suffragan Bishop of N. C., and acting in that office for all the Carolinas; the Rev. Dr. W. T. Hermitage who served nearly all his ministry in North Carolina, building churches and giving a son to the ministry.

Education was bringing about new class relationships within the Negro race itself as well as between the Negroes and the Whites; and upon these men and their associates devolved the task of adjusting these relationships. Wisely, with Christian patience and grace and faith, have they accepted the call and met the difficult duties. Looking back upon these forty years, it must fill the student of the story with admiration for these sane, steady, Christian leaders. Reflecting upon the great difficulties which beset them, surely only the most profound sympathy must be felt.

NOTE 13

(*Chapter VII, page 200*)

The story of Mr. Dodge is interesting, and his benefaction, in this region certainly, has but one parallel—that of Mr. Clarkson in South Carolina, which failed because of pre-war adverse laws.

Young Dodge came, about 1884, to visit his father, whose large interests were near Brunswick. The beauty of the surroundings, still with the scars of war apparent everywhere, the ruins of the old churches, the unshepherded Negroes wandering astray, the poverty from which recovery was necessarily slow—all these appealed to his fine sensibilities. He determined to apply for Holy Orders and devote himself to the Negro people of the islands. The story of Frederica Parish had been a romance; its ruin formed an irresistible appeal. On the foundation of the ruins he began to build, and, with the building, his vision enlarged to include the evangelization of some thirty-nine counties. After the earlier structures had been reared, he was ordained, and then proceeded to devote $72,000 to the Missions, of which he became Missionary Trustee with successive Rectors of Frederica as Trustees in turn. With the approval of the Bishop, he took over the Negro Mission work of the Diocese. One by one, Mission-Chapels (used often as schools during the week) were built, served sometimes by priests, sometimes by teachers who were also lay readers. The Rev Mr. Winn came first, as Assistant and remains in charge to this day.

One of the most noted of Mr. Dodge's Negro teachers was J. B. Gillespie, who went from the Sewanee St. Mark's Mission, in 1875, as lay reader of St. Perpetua Chapel and School, of which he was the first teacher. Gillespie's father had been chief of one of the black tribes of Africa. He was captured in battle and sold to one of the last slave-ships smuggling cargoes into America. In America, he came into the hands of Col. Peter Turney (afterwards Governor of Tennessee), a man of remarkable power and humanity. Gillespie was treated by the Colonel with due appreciation of his native standing. So Gillespie, the teacher, was a prince once removed from his native land; and he was one in character and in intellectual reach. Eventually he was ordained, intending to return to Africa as a Christian priest; but a fever epidemic through which he nursed his people, carried him away at its close, and he was buried by his chapel in 1887. The older people still revere his name.

NOTE 14

(*Chapter VII, page 207*)

The story of such establishments is not without its romance. These have been difficult to secure; but there are doubtless many more to parallel this tribute which is taken from *The Church Advocate*, of August, 1921. In the initial work leading to the foundation of Epiphany, Orange, Miss Ruth Mason was the moving spirit. She opened a Sunday School for the Negroes of the old parish, and has been a devoted friend and co-worker ever since. Says *The Advocate*, "In spite of her advanced age, she is worth more to the work in Orange than a

CURATE. IF WE ONLY HAD A FEW MORE SUCH IN EVERY NORTHERN COMMUNITY, CHURCH EXTENSION AMONG OUR GROUP IN SUCH LOCALITIES WOULD BECOME VITALLY REAL. MISS MASON WAS ALSO INSTRUMENTAL IN GETTING ST. ANDREW'S, PATTERSON, UNDER WAY."